MATRICIDE

The Denigration of the
American Women's Suffrage Movement

ISBN: 979-8-9896268-5-4

Printed and bound in the United States of America
by Ingram Lightning Source

Edited by: Jacque Hillman, Kim T. Stewart, Katie Gould
Cover design by: Jacque Hillman, Wanda Stanfill, Kim T. Stewart
Layout, design, and chapter art by: Kim T. Stewart

The HillHelen Group LLC
470 North Parkway, Suite C
Jackson, TN 38305

The HillHelen Group LLC
635 North 65th Place
Mesa, AZ 85205

(731) 394-2894
www.hillhelengrouppublishers.com
hillhelengroup@gmail.com

MATRICIDE

The Denigration of the
American Women's Suffrage Movement

Joanne M. Callahan

Praise for Joanne M. Callahan's
Matricide: The Denigration of the American Women's Suffrage Movement

"This book is not a whisper but a shout. We stand on the strong shoulders of those great suffragists who came before us. And where we go is up to us."

—Marguerite Kearns, granddaughter of suffragists Edna Buckman Kearns and Wilmer Kearns, and author of *An Unfinished Revolution: Edna Buckman Kearns and the Struggle for Women's Rights*

"This book is essential for anyone who cares about history and its proper representation. Women have always been overlooked for their contributions to our nation. Joanne Callahan has done a superb job of putting the Women's Suffrage Movement in the proper context with outstanding research and describing with numerous examples how suffragists' contributions are demeaned and trivialized. Highly recommended, because it's an incisive, enjoyable read."

—Paula F. Casey, co-founder of the Tennessee Woman Suffrage Heritage Trail and publisher of *The Perfect 36: Tennessee Delivers Woman Suffrage*

"*Matricide* makes an excellent case that great men always get a pass on their problematic views while suffragists are held to a different standard. The section titled 'What Made the Suffragists Great?' was a stroke of genius. I also appreciated the emphasis on the need for feminists to 'ripen the time' to guarantee that the Women's Suffrage Movement becomes a prominent part of American history instead of merely a footnote. Readers will come away armed with strategies for making that happen, something we need now more than ever."

—Misty Hook, PhD, licensed psychologist and former assistant professor of psychology, Texas Woman's University

"*Matricide* is a comprehensive, extensively researched, historical summary of the treatment of American suffragists. Though suffragists endured great hardship and surmounted incredible odds, historians have downplayed their amazing accomplishments in a manner not used on men.

"This disrespectful treatment leaves us to wonder how on earth the Nineteenth Amendment was ratified if what we are told by these historians has an ounce of truth. Kudos to Joanne M. Callahan for setting the record straight."

—Carol Donovan, 2015–2021 chairwoman, Dallas County Democratic Party

"Joanne Callahan makes a compelling argument that today's feminists frame suffragists and their sacrifices through internalized sexism and 'presentism'—holding historical figures to today's social standards.

"Rather, *Matricide* calls upon us to unapologetically celebrate suffragists' brilliance, sacrifices, achievements, and contributions to American democracy."

—Karen M. Kedrowski, PhD, professor of political science and director of the Carrie Chapman Catt Center for Women and Politics, Iowa State University

"*Matricide* embodies the power of celebrating the past. But Matricide does not stop there. The author documents current attitudes towards suffragists and how they impact the feminist movement. And *Matricide* offers specific steps we can take to let more women get a place at the table and come away satisfied."

—Linda M. Dedman, esquire, founder and CEO, Dedman Law PLLC

"In *Matricide*, Joanne Callahan calls on her personal experiences and observations to illustrate the ways suffragists have been misrepresented and underestimated by a hostile society and even sometimes by other women. Callahan's voice is clear and straightforward. She speaks out repeatedly in defense of both nuance and assertion in interpreting the Women's Suffrage Movement. Her suggestions, critiques, and ideas aim to push us forward in the right direction."

—Robert P. J. Cooney Jr., author of *Winning the Vote: The Triumph of the American Woman Suffrage Movement*

"In *Matricide*, Callahan provides an in-depth understanding of the sexism—on the part of women as well as men—that leads to women, including suffragists, being severely criticized, while men are celebrated."

—Myriam Miedzian, PhD, co-founder of Monumental Women, former professor of philosophy, and author of *Generations: A Century of Women Speak About Their Lives*

"*Matricide* is a call to action for historians to give equal space, forceful accolades, and proper recognition to the impact of the leaders who worked to get the Nineteenth Amendment passed."

—Cheryl Erb, board member of the Carrie Chapman Catt Girlhood Home and Museum, Charles City, Iowa

Suffragists march with signs showing the signatures of over one million New York women demanding to vote in October 1917.

Dedication

To our suffragist foremothers
in the United States
and around the world.
And to their male allies.

Attorney Sue Shelton White (holding Tennessee banner) and other activists picketed the Republican presidential nominating convention held in June 1920 in Chicago. Their sign accused Republicans of defeating ratification in Delaware and blocking ratification in Vermont and Connecticut.

Table of Contents

**Introduction: Remarkable but Flawed Women,
GREAT GREAT GREAT GREAT Men**   1

CHAPTER ONE

How Suffragists Get Denigrated   7

When the NYT Attacked the Suffrage Movement Twice,
and Women's History Groups Remained Silent   10

Put-Downs of Heroic Activists
Who Made the Ultimate Sacrifices   17
    Belittling Alice Paul in the Most Surprising Places   17
        Getting Canceled at the Alice Paul Center   19
        A Gray Day at the Belmont-Paul   26
    Dropping the Inez Milholland Campaign
    for the Presidential Citizens Medal   30
    Forgetting the Suffragists Abused by their Families   34
    Lauding Harry Burn While Ignoring Joseph Hanover   36
    Don't Mess with Texas Women—
    Unless They're Imprisoned Suffragists   40
    When Will the World Finally *Get It* About Lucy Burns?   47

The Protest March I Wanted to Start at Central Park   53

If We Really Want to Honor Black, Latina,
and Asian and Native American Suffragists   58

What Was Missing from that Tribute at Occoquan Park?   63

Suffs Gets My Vote, But Did It Really Honor the Suffragists? 67

CHAPTER TWO

Why Suffragists Get Denigrated   **71**

Racism, White Suffragists, 'Great Men,'
and the Double Standard   73
  The Suffragists' Legacy Is Complex, Evolving,
  and Always in Danger of Getting Forgotten   75
  Why Many Say White Suffragists Were Racists   77
  Why Many Say White Suffragists Were Not Racists   78
  What Did the Nineteenth Amendment
  Do for the Civil Rights Movement?   82
  The Questions We Need to Ask   84

The Vote vs. *The Agitators*: Who Has the Single Standard?   84

Suffragists and Faludi's Theory of Matricide   90

CHAPTER THREE

Fighting Back   **95**

Answering the Long-Overdue Question:
What Made the Suffragists Great?   96
  They Were Intellectually Brilliant   97
  They Were Phenomenal Innovators   102
  They Had Tremendous Political Acumen   105
  They Were Heroic   106

A Sign of Hope from Tennessee   108

Standing Up to Susan B. Anthony Pro-Life America   118

Carrie On   123

CHAPTER FOUR

Claiming Suffragists' True Place in History   **135**

Look in the Mirror   137

Fight Back When Suffragists Get
Patronized, Attacked, or Ignored   140

Resist When Second-Wave Feminists
Get Trashed or Canceled   142

Insist that Female Executives Honor
Their Suffragist and Feminist Foremothers   152

Ensure that Women's Suffrage Events Are Powerful   156

Show History Teachers How to Educate Students
About the Women's Suffrage Movement   162

Rebrand Women's Equality Day and
Call It Nineteenth Amendment Day   166

Do Women's History Activism on Nineteenth
Amendment Day and during Women's History Month   170
        Sow Winter Wheat for a Movement to Make
        Nineteenth Amendment Day a Federal Holiday   173

EPILOGUE   **179**

Endnotes   **183**

About the Author   **211**

Suffragists ride in a suffrage parade May 9, 1914, in Washington, DC, as male spectators keep to the sidewalk at left.

Activist Nannie Helen Burroughs, left, holds a sign reading, "Banner State Woman's National Baptist Convention," circa 1910. Burroughs helped found the Women's Convention of the National Baptist Convention. Burroughs, along with most members of the Women's Convention, was a staunch suffragist. She also held several leadership positions within the National Association of Colored Women (NACW).

Acknowledgments

Two years ago, I poured my heart out to Paula Casey, that irrepressible Tennessee suffrage history advocate, about the double standard of history, especially as it applies to suffragists and feminists. Without missing a beat, she suggested that I write a book. She then introduced me to her friend Jacque Hillman, senior editor and CEO of The HillHelen Group Publishers. Jacque believed in the project from the get-go. Without Paula and Jacque, it would never have occurred to me to write *Matricide*.

After I retired last year from a long career in information technology, I started to gather my thoughts. Every afternoon, I chuckled as I thought of well-meaning friends who urged me to "keep busy and don't let yourself get bored and depressed" after my exit from the corporate world. A few years ago, they were irritating, but I now see their point. The great thing about social activism is there's always something to do.

The works of John Blake and Susan Faludi provided invaluable guideposts as I worked on the book. Blake, with his succinct journalism and deep respect for the intricacies of history, showed me that it's OK to admit that the issue of racism in progressive white historical figures is complicated. Faludi's essay on the "matriciding" of previous generations of feminists provided an invaluable framework for understanding how the trashing of suffragists differs from garden variety misogyny. Her classic—and controversial—*Backlash: The Undeclared War Against American Women* was one of my templates for *Matricide*. Without Blake and Faludi, it would have been much harder to write this book.

My friends, Misty Hook and Linda Dedman, kept me going when it was hard to stay focused. All they had to do was ask, "How's the book coming?"

I am indebted to those who stood up to the canceling of suffragists: Myriam Miedzian, Ellen Goodman, Lynn Sherr, Karen M. Kedrowski, Robert P. J. Cooney Jr., and those who wrote protest letters to the *New York Times* and Iowa State University. It would have been near-impossible to write this book if I thought I was "the only one."

I never mentioned feminist art historians in *Matricide*, but I appreciate their brilliant insights on gender and art and the myriad ways they "turn the lights on." I hope that *Matricide* inspires them to write a book about the artistic representation of suffragists in statues and other memorials, and to critique current trends.

And a huge thank-you to two exceptional editors, Kim T. Stewart and Katie Gould, for putting up with me. Stewart is a great expert on the *Chicago Manual of Style,* and Gould made perceptive comments about the current political scene.

My deepest gratitude to Wanda Stanfill for her striking and wonderfully symbolic cover design. As long as yellow rose petals fly through the landscape, there is hope.

Joanne Callahan, August 5, 2025, Garland, Texas

The Senate of the Tennessee General Assembly at the moment the vote is called to ratify the Nineteenth Amendment. At the moment the last vote was tallied, and the Nineteenth Amendment was ratified in Tennessee, the suffragists standing in the balcony showered the legislators below with yellow rose petals. Despite those who predicted disaster as women claimed the right to vote, the South did not fall. Morality did not collapse.

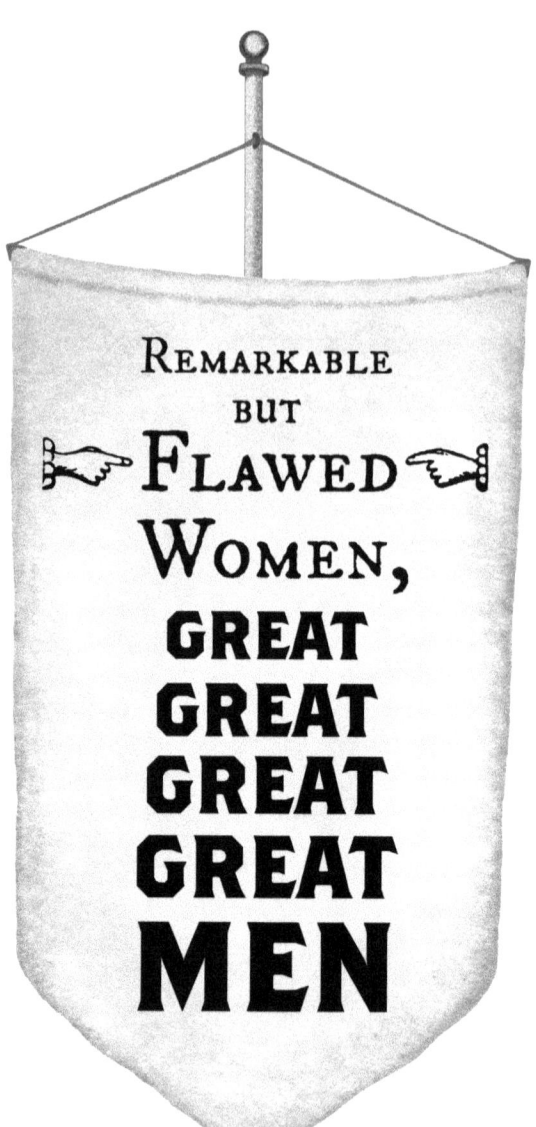

REMARKABLE
BUT
☞ FLAWED ☜
WOMEN,
GREAT
GREAT
GREAT
GREAT
MEN

"Had enough?"
Political advertisement

"I'm sick and tired of being sick and tired."
Fannie Lou Hamer, civil rights leader

"Write what should not be forgotten."
—Isabel Allende, novelist [1]

INTRODUCTION

During the 176th anniversary of the Seneca Falls Convention, I told a Methodist pastor that I was writing a book about the denigration of American suffragists. She looked shocked and responded, "But I am so grateful that we're finally getting statues and memorials. If we get critical, we will scare people off."

She agreed that the Seneca Falls Convention is one of the great moments in American history and was proud that the event was held at Wesleyan Methodist Chapel, where one hundred attendees boldly declared: "We hold these truths to be self-evident, that all men *and women* are created equal." She also thought the suffragists who went to prison were underrated American heroes. But she said she was too tired to promote these activists and changed the subject.

A few minutes after our conversation, I headed for the door. And then, the pastor tapped me on the shoulder.

"Too much gratitude can keep women down," she almost whispered.

"Yep, the gratitude trap," I chuckled.

Her comments brought flashbacks to the days when I was so thrilled that we were getting monuments that it never occurred to me that they could still denigrate these great activists. I thought naively that, at last, they would get the recognition they deserve and be lauded as great Americans. And yet, after eleven years of women's history advocacy, I have seen so much suffragist bashing that I feel an inner push to "write what should not be forgotten." I'm disgusted with the patronizing remarks about these great suffragists at unveilings of historical markers and statues. I am "sick and tired of being sick and tired" of the put-downs in articles, exhibits, movies, plays, and documentaries. I have had enough.

This disgust is buttressed by my experiences at places that honor the "great men of history." When I visited Normandy in 2013, I was stunned to see a "We welcome our liberators" sign *in English* at a restaurant in Bayeux. Everywhere I went, the Normandy veterans, both living and deceased, were treated like demigods. Several veterans have told me that while they are grateful that the Allied soldiers' sacrifices have not been forgotten, the accolades are overwhelming.

Indeed, not all our soldiers were angels in uniform. When historian Mary Louise Roberts published a critically acclaimed book[2] showing that our boys were not the knights of our fantasies and that a few were guilty of conduct unbecoming, several readers immediately went on the attack.[3] It was hardly a shock during Christiane Amanpour's podcast on the eightieth anniversary of D-Day that we heard nothing about the veterans' flaws, and everyone praised the "Greatest Generation."[4]

Likewise, when I toured Soweto in 2019, a twenty-one-year-old guide shouted out, "Nelson Mandela freed me." He never mentioned other great anti-apartheid activists, nor did he give any credit to allies around the world. Every room in Mandela's house was full of praise for the legendary activist. We heard nothing about his shortcomings as a husband and father and as president of South Africa.

When the *Economist* noted that younger South Africans are questioning Mandela's legacy, the magazine admitted that "it does South Africans no favours to elevate anyone to cult-like status." But the *Economist* immediately warned us that "there is a danger of inaccurate revisionism."[5]

In contrast, when I explored Seneca Falls in 2015 and toured the Elizabeth Cady Stanton House, the guide was all too quick to point out her personal and political flaws. I heard about her discipline problems with her older sons, but almost nothing about her remarkable son Theodore and her brilliant daughter Harriot Stanton Blatch.

She never mentioned that Theodore was an esteemed *Associated Press* journalist in Paris and that he advocated for women to compete in the Olympics. [6] She dutifully mentioned that Harriot was a suffragist but never added that her superb leadership helped reignite American suffrage activism in the 1910s.

The guide couldn't resist telling us that Stanton made nasty remarks about Irish immigrants. But she ignored the fact that Stanton also supported Irish Home Rule and admired the legendary Irish nationalist, Daniel O'Connell. [7]

When the guide finally got around to talking about Stanton's feminism, she admitted that her groundbreaking contributions were remarkable, which prompted an audience member to say, "She must have been a really intelligent woman."

After being a "good girl" for way too long, I instantly pushed back: "You would have never been so condescending if Stanton had been a man. Elizabeth Cady Stanton was a genius, and she was a lot more than remarkable."

This "emphasize their flaws and understate their brilliance" approach to suffragists has been repeated so many times that I am writing this deeply personal book in hopes that it will ignite a much-needed course correction, and that we will finally start to escape from the gratitude trap.

There are so many problems with the "great man" theory of history. The achievements of legendary male leaders are highly overstated. Nevertheless, military and civil rights groups learned long, long ago that if they don't honor the accomplishments of the past, men and women are not going to be motivated to do the hard work of fighting wars and advocating racial justice in the future.

Likewise, if we keep "matriciding" the Women's Suffrage Movement and other historic feminist accomplishments, the women's movement will eventually get weaker. Fewer women are going to do the hard work of feminist activism if they keep seeing a pattern of accomplishments getting denigrated fifty to one hundred years later by the people benefitting from them, even when we build monuments to them. I have lost a lot of enthusiasm for doing women's rights work because of the trashing of suffragists.

Pro-democracy advocates around the world are dealing with the fact that the United States is becoming more authoritarian, that women's rights are going backwards, and that there is an onslaught of misogyny among young men. Thus it is crucial to honor women's suffragists as beacons in the storm not only to build morale but to show the world that we are NOT going to forget their heroic sacrifices and squander their legacy. Never forget that in the age of Donald Trump, those who want to repeal the Nineteenth Amendment are getting out of the shadows.

When I got the news about the defeated Kamala Harris campaign—where, in the words of political commentator Van Jones, "He gets to be lawless. She has to be flawless." [8]—I wondered if I should put this book on hold. It is going to take countless volunteer hours for all of us to protect the remaining guardrails of American democracy.

I knew from the get-go that several campaign problems had nothing to do with sexism and racism, beginning with Merrick Garland's slow start of the January 6th investigation. But when Adam Roberts of the *Economist* said that he didn't buy the view that sexism played a role in the outcome of the election,[9] and when Richard Reeves said, "Sexism is too easy a story for the Democrats to tell themselves,"[10] an inner voice shouted out, "Forward march."

When I heard that men in college dorms were crowing, "Your body, my choice, forever," there was no turning back.

During the election, I made phone calls to independent swing-state voters for the Harris/Walz ticket. The Adam Roberts and Richard Reeves types won't believe it, but a few people asked me, "Is this country ready for a woman?" Even after Harris trounced Trump in a debate, one man wondered if she could stand up to Putin. Misogynoir is not the whole cause of her defeat, but it played a role. Full stop.

So here I am, writing a book about the denigration of American suffragists while trying to do my part to keep extreme, right-wing authoritarians from destroying "a terrible beauty"—a ravishing, indispensable nation that my Irish and Italian ancestors emigrated to in the nineteenth and early twentieth centuries. [11]

But as feminist theorist Cynthia Enloe stated:

"History is not just about 'yesterday.' It is about today—and tomorrow. How we craft our personal and our collective memories shapes how we imagine ourselves in the world today. That, in turn, will influence how we feel and act tomorrow." [12]

LEFT: Komako Kimura, a Japanese suffragist, participates in a march in New York in 1917. Kimura was an actress, dancer, and magazine editor. Her work shaped the women's rights and suffrage movement in Japan.

RIGHT: Jovita Idar was a Mexican-American journalist and activist who often faced dangerous situations. She single-handedly protected her newspaper headquarters when the Texas Rangers came to shut it down, and crossed the border to serve as a nurse during the Mexican Revolution. Idar, a resolute suffragist, was the founding president of La Liga Femenil Mexicanista (The League of Mexican Women). She exhorted women to recognize their rights, raise up their chins, and face the fight.

How Suffragists Get DENIGRATED

"First of all, nobody gave us anything. It makes me furious when I hear that they gave us suffrage."
Gerda Lerner, pioneering feminist historian [1]

"There can be only one winner—men—when 'white feminists' are attacked by other women."
Sonia Sodha, columnist, the *Guardian* [2]

"My silences had not protected me. Your silence will not protect you."
Audre Lorde, poet, feminist political theorist [3]

CHAPTER ONE

When four conservative Republican women senators declared, "This Monument Has Been Missing from the Mall Far Too Long" in the *Washington Post* [4] during Women's History Month 2024, I wondered, "How in the world will people ever believe that suffragists are still getting denigrated?"

Their description of the bipartisan campaign to place a Women's Suffrage National Monument on the National Mall was a refreshing change from the usual Washington polarization. It was also a reminder of how far we have come since 1921, when congressmen dumped the Portrait Monument statue of Elizabeth Cady Stanton, Susan B. Anthony, and Lucretia Mott into the basement below the Rotunda after it had been unveiled, and the media remained silent. [5]

Moreover, it was a reminder of the successful campaign for the Portrait Monument in the 1990s, when several congressmen didn't want to put the statue back on the Rotunda because they thought the suffragists were ugly. [6] Feminist congresswomen pushed back with biting wit and won.

Those of us who were around at that time have never forgotten when Patricia Schroeder told her colleagues in her usual cheeky way, "George Washington was hardly a ten." [7] Carolyn Maloney dryly quipped, "Lincoln wasn't placed in the Rotunda because of his good looks." [8]

Nevertheless, I have mountains of evidence that suffragists are still getting denigrated. My conviction is based on years of observation and research: volunteering with the National Votes for Women Trail, participating in marker unveilings in Texas, visiting memorials in almost every region of the country, watching movies and TV series, reading numerous articles, and seeing *Suffs* on Broadway. The proof is out there.

Indeed, after seeing so many historic memorials around the world, I have concluded that they usually fall into these categories:

- **Idolize:** These memorials usually treat a historic figure like a demigod and explain away his flaws. Almost all these idolized figures are men. When a liberal Lutheran pastor told me with complete certainty that Martin Luther King would be completely non-sexist if he had lived during second- and third-wave feminism, I said, "That's idolatry, darlin.'" I have never seen suffragists idolized.

- **Honor:** These memorials treat a historic figure with admiration and admit his or her flaws, but they view the person's achievement as "the whole is greater than its parts." To honor, say, Alice Paul is to call her a great activist and list her limitations but admit that she deserves as much recognition as the "great men of history." A few suffragists get honored, but they don't get honored enough.

• **Acknowledge:** These memorials list a person's achievements, but they don't show any admiration, and they never say that she deserves as much respect as the "great men of history." They make sure that we know the person's flaws. It often feels like the memorial is trying to keep us from admiring her. Most suffrage memorials are in the Acknowledge category.

• **Trash:** These memorials emphasize a person's flaws and are understated about her achievements. Sometimes, they don't mention what made that person great. During the 2019 Women's March in Dallas, a history professor at a local community college said that Susan B. Anthony was on the wrong side of history because she didn't want Frederick Douglass to speak at a suffrage convention in Atlanta. This historian gave no historical context and never listed Anthony's stunning achievements. She was guilty of trashing, an all-too-common occurrence when people talk about suffragists.

These categories are intended as basic guidelines, not hard and fast rules. I have no taste for making them more granular or developing a classification system. Regardless, I am concerned that the proposed Capitol Mall monument will not honor the suffragists, and that they will get patronized at best, insulted at worst, during the unveiling. I have seen too many women's history groups fall into the gratitude trap and the poverty mentality to feel confident about future suffrage memorials doing justice to these great activists.

In hopes of avoiding these problems in the future, I will report on my disappointing and sometimes devastating experiences with women's suffrage memorials in this section. I could easily provide an infinite number of examples. In the interest of brevity, I will cover only the standouts I saw from 2018 to October 2024, along with commentary on *Suffs*.

When the NYT Attacked the Suffrage Movement, and Women's History Groups Remained Silent

I had a lot of fun doing women's history activism in 2018. I was volunteering for the National Votes for Women Trail (NVWT)[9] and loved its just-do-it approach to publicizing famous and forgotten "suffs" of all races and classes from every state in the union. I was impressed with the fact that the group had built a sizable suffrage sites database on a shoestring[10] and allowed laypeople like me to update it—on the condition that I had accurate information.

But while I was getting so many exciting stories about great, forgotten Texas suffragists and updating the NVWT database, I stumbled upon Brent Staples's *New York Times* bombshell: "How the Suffrage Movement Betrayed Black Women."[11]

Like most articles about racism in the suffrage movement, this one accused white suffragists in broad brushstrokes of selling out to white supremacy so that they could advance their agenda. It prominently quoted Elizabeth Cady Stanton's offensive "Sambo" slur against Black men, but it also put Frederick Douglass on a pedestal and ignored the sexist remarks he made to her and Susan B. Anthony.

The article disregarded the precarious political environment that suffragists had to work in, and it brushed off the fact that all activists, including civil rights leaders, have had to play realpolitik to get laws passed.[12] Moreover, it ignored the fact that during the Civil War, Stanton and Anthony put women's rights activism on hold and devoted all their political energy to abolitionism.

However, what separated Staples's work from other like-minded articles was its insulting divide-and-conquer assertion that "white women were seeking the vote as a symbol of parity with their husbands and brothers. Black women, most of whom lived in the South, were seeking the ballot for themselves and their men, as a means of empowering Black communities besieged by the reign of racial terror that erupted after Emancipation." [13]

I completely agree with Staples about the deep racial terror that engulfed this country after the Civil War. Nevertheless, he had no respect for the fact that numerous white women of all classes, religions, and ethnic groups became suffragists because they realized through painful experiences that without a vote, they have no voice, and that they are at the mercy of their fathers, husbands, sons, bosses, and political leaders. Symbolism had very little to do with it.

And that's when I suspected that Staples's article was part of a smear campaign. I was not the only one who had such "bad" thoughts. The article's comments section backed me up:

> I am a former teacher of African American history, and can thus tell you that Mr. Staples only has the story partially right. It is more nuanced than he states.
>
> —Sierra [14]

> Looking forward to the editorial on the ways the Civil Rights Movement, and other Black rights movements, betrayed women as well . . .
>
> —LLS [15]

> Activists today who promote conflict between Black rights and women's rights to the extent that they feel the need to question the motivations for the Nineteenth Amendment are working towards the result of negating them both.
>
> —ERP [16]

However, I didn't see any comments from women's history groups. A few days later, I did notice a rebuke from Elizabeth Cady Stanton's great-great-granddaughter.

Coline Jenkins's short rebuttal bluntly stated that Staples was wrong about Stanton being a "classical liberal racist" and that "[her] lifetime of action supporting rights for African Americans speaks louder than her angry outburst after female suffrage was denied." [17] She noted that "Frederick Douglass attested more than once to the strength and solace he found in her presence. The respect was mutual." [18]

I'm glad Jenkins sent the letter, but it takes more than one gunshot to stop an attack when a hundred tanks are on their way. I never heard a discussion about the threat posed by the Brent Staples article during NVWT calls or in any women's history articles. When I asked about it, people would either change the subject or refer to Jenkins's letter. Yes, the silence was partly because of denial and a fear of betraying intersectional principles, but it was also because we were all so busy planning the festivities for the Nineteenth Amendment Centennial. We were preparing new historical markers and statues and getting ready for parties. We were publicizing new books, documentaries, and lectures and were so excited about the possibility that finally, suffragists would get the respect they deserve.

I was delighted when the William G. Pomeroy Foundation awarded the National Collaborative for Women's History Sites—which has NVWT as one of its major projects—a commission to place beautiful historical markers on suffrage sites in every state in the country. [19] I was helping our Texas team get markers for Lone Star suffragists and was starting to view the NYT article as no more than a bump in the road.

By December 2019, I was getting so optimistic about the Nineteenth Amendment Centennial that I had forgotten about the Staples smear. I was elated when I finally received approval for a marker at Dallas's historic Millermore Mansion [20] honoring the suffragist leader Nona Boren Mahoney and the politician Barry Miller. [21] The NVWT was thrilled about our plan to unveil it during the popular Jazz Age festival in March 2020, and I had bought a flapper costume for the occasion.

We all know what happened in March. Dallas, along with the rest of the world, got torpedoed by COVID. On May 25, George Floyd was killed, and Black Lives Matter activists started marching in the streets.

We unveiled the Nona Boren Mahoney marker in August 2020 with twenty masked, socially distanced people in the audience, a far cry from the fifteen hundred we had envisioned at the rollicking Jazz Age festival.

And then, NYT sent in the tanks. The Brent Staples article was an insult, but the article from the editorial board was a slap in the mouth, one of the most vicious examples of the weaponization of history that I have ever read in the mass media. (Yes, I know all about NYT and the *1619 Project*.)

"The 19th Amendment: An Important Milestone in an Unfinished Journey," posted on August 15, 2020,[22] focused on the unsung leadership of Black suffragists but played the divide-and-conquer game. It denigrated Elizabeth Cady Stanton and Susan B. Anthony as self-serving and completely ignored Alice Paul, Lucy Burns, and numerous other women who protested at the White House and were tortured in prison.

The editorial implied that the movement was a stroll in the park for affluent Anglo-Saxon Protestant women. It ignored the fact that there was a long, grueling struggle for all suffragists—and that success was never guaranteed.

The editorial board saved its most violent statements for the last paragraph: "The Nineteenth Amendment can fairly be seen as an important milestone in an unfinished journey. It is morally repugnant and counterproductive to mythologize it as a triumph of egalitarianism . . ."[23]

Fortunately, there was a huge uproar in the article comments:

> I am in favor of exploring the history of the Women's Suffrage Movement, including the role racism played. But it's incredibly frustrating—indeed, "morally repugnant"—when a decades-long, serious political

movement—one for which women died—is tacitly characterized as one of "privileged" white women holding silly parades.

—Laura[24]

It's "morally repugnant" to celebrate any step along a journey except the last one? The *Times* should be ashamed of itself for denigrating the Nineteenth Amendment, which was, in absolute fact, a tremendous milestone.

—Green Tea[25]

I expect if on the sixtieth anniversary of the Voting Rights Act, op-ed writers denounced the Civil Rights Movement and its leaders for being so biased for focusing so extensively on Black voting rights over other social issues—and dismissing the value of a figure like Martin Luther King Jr.—there would be outrage. . . . This pathetic screed is not even worthy of a C in a tenth-grade history class.

—JD[26]

The NYT has spent the entire year minimizing the accomplishments of the suffrage movement and its leaders. Their work has been not only incredibly biased but often historically inaccurate. I hope anyone seeking to learn the history of this powerful movement seeks a more impartial source, because they will certainly not find it in this paper.

—JD[27]

But what did women's history groups say? Nothing. Absolutely nothing. I know they couldn't afford to publish a full-page protest in the NYT, but I felt betrayed when the National Votes for Women Trail, the National Women's History Alliance, Susan B. Anthony Museum, and other women's history groups didn't write protest letters.

I got the usual denials when I tried to talk about the screed: I didn't see it. We're too busy catching up on marker approvals and unveilings because of the COVID setback. But the NYT had a great pictorial history of the Women's Suffrage Movement. You're too negative.

Some people asked me to send them a link to the article, but I never heard their comments about it.

I searched a long time for criticism of the editorial, but I found only two articles: Myriam Miedzian's "The Suffragists Were Not Racists, So Cancel the Cancel Culture and Celebrate an Accusation-Free Suffrage Centennial" and Ellen Goodman and Lynn Sherr's "The Mother of All Celebrations."

The Miedzian article does not reference the NYT editorial, but it punches holes in the writers' source material, especially when they claimed that Stanton and Anthony ignored the contributions of Black suffragists in the *History of Woman Suffrage*:

> Wrong. The first three volumes by Stanton and Anthony contain eighty-five references to Black suffragists. Some of their speeches are quoted extensively. Considering that Black women made up six percent of the population, this represents an impressive number.[28]

Ellen Goodman and Lynn Sherr's "The Mother of All Celebrations" started by expressing the dashed hopes of women and men around the country:

> This is not how we thought we'd be celebrating the one hundredth anniversary of American women's right to vote. We figured confetti and cocktails, triumphant

gatherings of women and men. White pantsuits and
a red rose . . .[29]

They detailed how the celebrations got torpedoed by COVID and
the cancel culture. And then, they shot back at the NYT screed:

> One hostile rap on the festivities comes from the *New
> York Times*, whose recent editorial calls celebrating
> this giant step towards equality "morally repugnant."
> Curiously, the writers ignore the historically repugnant
> fact that their own newspaper adamantly opposed
> suffrage.[30]

It was gratifying to see forceful pushback. But when women's
history groups were so silent, I knew that NYT and other media
outlets would not think twice before firing another shot. Attackers are
deterred by large, organized groups. Scattered masses of individuals?
Not so much.

My enthusiasm for women's history activism took a deep nosedive
in 2020 mainly because of media attacks on suffragists and the silence
of women's history groups. While I still did volunteer work, I now
feared that those efforts were a waste of time. One reader's reaction,
posted by "Anja" in the comments section of Brent Staples's article,
certainly applied to me:

> I am genuinely afraid that obscuring the notable work
> of the suffrage movement by somehow scraping to find
> fatal flaws within the positions of some of its founders
> will only serve to stall the progress we have made as
> feminists and progressives.[31]

But I got a ray of hope, because I had discovered the Alice Paul
Institute (API).

Put-Downs of Heroic Activists
Who Made the Ultimate Sacrifices

When I was in elementary school, the priests and sisters often told us stories about the sacrifices of early Christians and Catholic saints. They quoted from John 15:13 in the Christian Scriptures: "Greater love has no man than this: that a man lay down his life for his friends." [32]

They made sure we honored their sacrifices, and they had zero tolerance for trashing. I learned very early that "honor their sacrifices" didn't apply only to religious martyrs. My parents, friends, relatives, teachers, and the media burned into my brain the idea that the sacrifices of military leaders like Eisenhower and WWII resistance legends like Jean Moulin must never be forgotten or trivialized.

When I lived in Birmingham, Alabama, from 2002 to 2004 and visited civil rights memorials throughout the South, the "honor their sacrifices" philosophy was up close and in plain sight. Sister Rita Ellen (not her real name) primed me perfectly for it. On the day after Martin Luther King was shot, she quoted from the Gospel of John and told all of us to stand in silence in honor of his martyrdom.

Unfortunately, "honor their sacrifices" often lapsed into idolatry, especially when the honorees were men. But it would have been equally unfair if their sacrifices had been ignored or just acknowledged.

After seeing *Iron Jawed Angels* in 2005 and hearing women tell me that they started voting because they were so stunned by the suffragists' sacrifices, I thought we were on the way to treating them with the honor they deserved. When I heard that an institute was named after Alice Paul and that a new museum was named after Lucy Burns, I was elated.

But reality set in quickly.

Belittling Alice Paul in the Most Surprising Places

I strongly believe—without apology—that Alice Paul deserves as much recognition as Martin Luther King, Mahatma Gandhi, and Nelson Mandela. Her genius as an organizer and a publicist and her heroism are indisputable. When Cory Booker said on Instagram that "Alice Paul is an American hero who [sic] we don't recognize or celebrate enough," he got no argument from me, especially when he praised "the artistry of the suffragists' activism." [33]

My experiences have led me to guesstimate that 95 percent of the American public, including many feminists, liberals, and progressives, know nothing about Alice Paul. Thus, I feel compelled to tell the world about her outstanding accomplishments.

Paul, along with Lucy Burns, organized the groundbreaking 1913 Suffrage Parade in Washington, DC. She was the architect of the innovative White House protests, and of the brilliant Prison Special train tour in which women who had been imprisoned for activism traveled throughout the United States building support for women's rights. She had a rare gift for keeping the suffrage issue on the front page and holding politicians' feet to the fire, including President Wilson.

Paul was imprisoned three times in Britain and another three times in the United States for demanding that these nations stop denying women their natural right to vote. She was put into solitary confinement in an American prison and was almost committed to an insane asylum. In interviews towards the end of her life, her view of the violence she suffered reminded me of the recollections of resistance fighters during WWII. She was stoic almost to the point of denial, except when she talked about Dr. William A. White:

> He wouldn't in any way consent to have me transferred to St. Elizabeth [insane asylum] ... So I have always felt the greatest sense of indebtedness to him. And so I am afraid I might have stayed there forever—like many, many, many, many, many women over the country. [34]

Radicals make movements move. Without a brilliant militant like Alice Paul, suffragists probably would have had to fight for several more years, or even decades, to get an amendment into the Constitution.

Paul could have retired from activism after 1920, but her heart was always with women's rights. Convinced that a state-by-state approach could never eradicate the deep sexism in our legal system, she introduced the Equal Rights Amendment to Congress in 1923.

Alarmed by anti-feminist backlash and fascist threats in Europe, she founded the World Woman's Party in Switzerland in 1938. She lived in Geneva until 1941 and urged the League of Nations to make women's rights a top priority.

As Nazi terror edged closer to the Swiss border, Paul devoted all her time to sheltering Jewish refugees and helping them get visas to come to the United States as quickly as possible. [35]

After WWII, Paul worked diligently with feminists around the world to stamp women's rights into the United Nations Charter and the 1948 Universal Declaration of Human Rights. She kept advocating for the ERA. She insisted on including sex discrimination in Title VII of the Civil Rights Act of 1964 and triumphed, along with other feminists, against stringent opposition.

Alice Paul had her flaws. So did MLK, Gandhi, and Mandela. But, to paraphrase Dolly Parton, Paul's mistakes are no worse than theirs just because she is a woman.

Getting Canceled at the Alice Paul Center

When I discovered the Alice Paul Institute in August 2020, it was almost like an answered prayer. Their free Zoom calls during the height of the pandemic lifted my morale, and at first the institute seemed like it was tailor-made for a fan like me.

API had a clever online wine-tasting fundraiser; inspiring discussions with activist Martha Burke and Sen. Cory Booker; an eye-opening presentation on Joseph Hanover, the Jewish Tennessee state representative who got death threats and anti-Semitic slurs because of his strong political leadership on the Nineteenth Amendment; and edifying conversations about the 2020 presidential election.

API continued this train of excellence in 2021 and 2022. Einav Rabinovitch-Fox did a fun presentation on the powerful impact of suffragists and feminists on fashion designers. Rebecca DeWolf introduced us to *Gendered Citizenship*, her fascinating book about ERA activism from the 1920s to 1963. Steve Anderson gave a delightful address on Republicans for ERA (yes, they still exist!), and Jane Rosenberg gave a superb lecture on the life of Pauli Murray.

But in 2021, I started to notice trouble in this online paradise. During Alice Paul's birthday celebration in January, they showed the film, *Without a Whisper*, and then, Wakerakatste Louise McDonald Herne and Dr. Sally Roesch Wagner gave a lecture about the influence of Native American women on the suffrage movement and the oppression of Native Americans in the nineteenth and early twentieth centuries.

The Trail of Tears is a crucial topic, but why in the world did they discuss it on Alice Paul's birthday? They could have easily focused on it during Native American Heritage Month. I strongly doubt that they would have discussed the oppression of South African women and LGBTIQ+ individuals in the apartheid era during a birthday celebration for Nelson Mandela. Nobody would stand for treating a "great man of history" so badly.

After the birthday celebration, I noticed that, like almost all suffragist websites, the API webpage description of Alice Paul was too modest about her accomplishments. [36] For starters, the "Feminist. Suffragist. Political Strategist" subtitle should have said, "Brilliant Political Strategist. Outstanding Suffragist Leader. Groundbreaking Feminist." A concise summary of *all of Paul's major accomplishments throughout her life* should have been in the first two or three paragraphs. It wouldn't have hurt to include a few accolades from Cory Booker and other eminent scholars and political leaders.

When I voiced my concerns to API management, they told me that Alice Paul was a modest Quaker who didn't like it when people bragged about her, and that API is not an Alice Paul museum.

It's not terribly inspiring to treat an activist who deserves as much recognition as the "great men of history" like she was just a "remarkable but flawed woman." Basically, it perpetuates the double standard. API could have continued its leadership programs for girls and young women and its ERA advocacy while making sure that the world recognizes her as a great leader.

From time to time, I was getting strange vibes about the institute. After Heather Sharkey, a professor at the University of Pennsylvania, gave an excellent presentation on "The Mystery of Alice Paul's Missing Dissertation," she asked why Alice Paul is such a polarizing figure in the twenty-first century. Most tellingly, nobody gave any answers. A few days later, I got an insight into why she wanted to start that discussion. I found out that in September 2021, Alice Paul had gotten canceled at the university. The Alice Paul Center was renamed the Center for Research in Feminist, Queer, and Transgender Studies. As far as I know, there was never a public debate, and I never got any message about the issue from API.

In its close embrace of intersectionality, almost every API presentation on women's suffrage reminded us of racism within the movement, which initially didn't bother me. However, I got miffed when presenters sometimes acted like they would have triumphantly stood up to Southern white racists if they had been in Alice Paul's shoes. They had very little sense of the precarious political environment suffragists had to work in.

I also got irritated because the presenters almost never talked about sexism and misogyny in the Abolitionist and Civil Rights movements. Those of us who called out that double standard got dinged by the program coordinators, even when a few audience members defended us.

When Paige Harrington gave a presentation on "The Legacy of Women's Suffrage at Museums and Historic Sites" on Alice Paul's birthday in 2022 and focused intensely on racism, I skipped out. I later watched it on YouTube and thought it was pretty good, especially when she talked about how difficult it is to have productive conversations about racism. But it wasn't an appropriate topic for a birthday celebration. Again, the double standard.

In a culture where most Americans know nothing about Alice Paul, and those of us who admire her are tired of educating people about her, it would have been more helpful if API had done what birthday celebrations are supposed to do: Honor the outstanding and deeply human activist without idolizing her. API could have had great presentations on:

- **"Teaching Children, Teens, and Undergrads about Alice Paul and the Suffrage Movement"**: Middle school, high school, and undergrad college history professors describe their experiences and give tips and tricks on getting the message across in a hostile or indifferent environment.

- **"History Textbooks and the Sticky Floor"**: Why it's so difficult for Alice Paul historians and advocates to get a foot in the door with history textbook publishers, and what "we the people" can do about it.

- **"When Will the Movies Get It on Alice Paul?"**: Feminist film critics give their take on *Iron Jawed Angels* and *Mrs. America*. They discuss why the stylish series about Phyllis Schlafly, Gloria Steinem, and other ERA activists (both pro and anti) completely ignored her.

- **"Alice Paul's Leadership Techniques"**: J. D. Zahniser and other Alice Paul biographers give insights into what made her a great leader and what we can learn from her. They also discuss her limitations.

- **"Idolatry, Honor, Acknowledgment, Trashing"**: What is the difference between idolizing historical leaders, honoring them, merely acknowledging them, and trashing them? How can API challenge the double standard of history?

As the year 2022 progressed, I drifted away from API partly because of a troublesome statement in the Code of Conduct, which the program coordinator read at the beginning of every online call: "If anyone chooses to engage in racist, sexist, trans or homophobic speech, or any other kind of harassment or bullying behavior, ***they will be removed from the program without further warning.***"[37]

Yes, you heard it right: They will be removed from the program without further warning. They didn't give people a chance to repent with a "three strikes and you're out" policy; they didn't provide a list of what speech they consider racist, sexist, transphobic, and homophobic; and they themselves used sexist language. I cringed when presenters and API staff called women "guys" and said, "Women were given the vote."[38]

I hate to say it, but that speech code experience made me think of conservative critics of wokeness and political correctness. Did they have a point? It also reminded me of moderate, liberal, and feminist academics who admitted the left has gotten too extreme and told young people that it's not worth it to pursue a career in academia anymore.

By the time 2023 rolled around, I withdrew from the group but stayed on as a passive Facebook follower. Nevertheless, I still thought, "Someday, when I'm close to the Mount Laurel, New Jersey, area, I want to visit API so that I can pay my respects and see Alice Paul's gorgeous family home."

That opportunity came in the fall of 2024, when I was planning to see *Suffs* in New York. Since API does not accept drop-ins for tours (which it holds only on Thursday through Sunday), I called and made an appointment two weeks before my trip. I had a pleasant chat with a staff member who helped me choose the most efficient subway route from New York.

However, the conversation started to go south when I said I was excited about visiting API but was offended during the Alice Paul birthday celebrations in 2021 and 2022. I added that Mandela would NEVER be treated like that on his birthday. The staff member said something like, "People treat famous activists like gods and that is a big problem, so we are committed to telling the whole story about Alice Paul, warts and all."

The staff member added, "We recently changed our name to the Alice Paul Center for Gender Justice." I was so surprised that I blurted, "Well, sex is biological, and gender is sociological."

The staff member vehemently disagreed and started talking about the intersexed and the transgendered. I listened, and then I mentioned that I had read articles about people who had detransitioned because it had affected their physical health. The staff member ended the conversation and emailed me a map and a link to the "About the Alice Paul Center" page, where I saw this description of the great activist:

> We continually reckon with understanding the *flawed and nuanced life* of Alice Paul as she at once fought for gender equality and excluded Black suffragists in that journey. We affirm that no oppressed group is truly fighting for emancipation if it liberates itself while leaving others in their chains. [39]

There is a lot to unpack in that vituperative paragraph, but the phrase that gobsmacked me was "flawed and nuanced life."

Flawed and nuanced life?? What the @#$%^????? If any staff member at Mount Vernon and Monticello wrote that Washington and Jefferson had led "flawed and nuanced lives," that person would get fired. *That statement was beyond insulting. It essentially canceled Alice Paul while benefitting from her legacy.* But I said nothing, because I knew I would get knocked down.

Shortly before I left for New York, I called the center to make sure that I had correctly interpreted the map that the staff member had sent me, especially since the trip takes three hours. I had a nice conversation with the staffer, who told me that I would get an email soon.

One hour later, Rachael Glashan Rupisan, the executive director, sent me a cancelation because of "repetitive misconduct of our policies."[40] She underlined the Code of Conduct statement, "Be respectful. Use kind words and respectful speech. Don't be abusive, hostile, or threatening to others."[41]

In my response to Rupisan, I said, "I was shocked by this email. In what way have I performed repetitive misconduct of your policies? Please give some details."[42] She never replied.

There is nothing abusive, hostile, or threatening about saying, "Sex is biological; gender is sociological," or noting that some people have detransitioned because it impacted their physical health. No, I do not think those statements are transphobic.[43] When I said I was offended by the Alice Paul birthday celebrations, I was not trashing the Alice Paul Center, especially since I also admitted that I was excited about visiting the historic landmark.

I was the latest victim of cancel culture. I was shocked, angry, and sad. I felt betrayed. If anyone had told me in 2020 that API was going to cancel me in 2024, I would have laughed at that person's right-wing paranoia. Why in the world would they cancel an Alice Paul fan like me?

I'd like to say that the story is over, but a few days after Thanksgiving, I got a snail-mail from—you guessed it—Rachael Glashan Rupisan. Even though the salutation said, "Dear Joanne," it was a form letter. And, yes, it asked for money. But Rupisan made several knockout comments that reminded me of my happiest moments at API:

> **We are living in a moment of profound crisis for women's rights.** The progress our mothers and grandmothers fought so hard to achieve faces unprecedented threats . . . it strikes at the very heart of women's status as full citizens of our democracy . . .
>
> Our predecessors—suffragists, civil rights activists, and feminist pioneers—did not merely leave us a legacy. **They left us a mandate.** They showed us how to fight . . . Now it is our turn to take up their torch.[44]

Wow! Those statements were so powerful that I started thinking, "Perhaps I shouldn't write the center off. Maybe I should keep trying to dialogue with the leaders."

However, the letter flopped when Rupisan said, "Our role becomes even more vital by preserving the authentic history that others would diminish or deny."[45] Sorry, but after four years of involvement at API and the Alice Paul Center, I have seen too much diminishment of the quiet Quaker Jersey girl who became one of the greatest activists of the twentieth century. I do not trust the Alice Paul Center to preserve, promote, and defend her legacy.

In 2020 and 2021, I happily donated to API, but after that devastating cancel culture experience, the center will get no funds from me. I have moved on, especially since I got good support from feminist friends. But this experience will hang over every activist decision I make for the rest of my life.

A Gray Day at the Belmont-Paul

When I opened the backyard door of the Belmont-Paul (BP) Women's Equality National Monument in Washington, DC, in 2024, my arms were all wet. I had walked for several blocks in the splattering September rain and my Orvis raincoat wasn't up to the task.

As I walked to the front desk, the park rangers told me that the air conditioning wasn't working in the exhibit rooms, and they looked discouraged. These problems kept me from taking a guided tour, and I braced myself for disappointment.

But I went to the exhibits anyway—with frequent breaks to the freezing library room. It felt like I was switching from the equator to the polar ice cap. I had heard that the BP had a video, but I never saw it. On the front door of the house, the overhead fanlight with the bright blue Tiffany design was stunning. But all the rooms were dark because of the overcast weather. A friend told me that on sunny days, the house is much brighter and a lot more impressive.

Even though the overcast weather didn't show BP at its best, I could still see that it is a lovely historic home. BP has many interesting artifacts and photos, and the historic landmark certainly makes up for the threadbare treatment of the Women's Suffrage Movement in our American history textbooks. BP gave a good overview of the movement from 1848 to 1920 and of the ERA campaign from 1920 to 2020. The monument emphasized Alva Belmont and Alice Paul's contributions and acknowledged the suffragists' innovations. The exhibits at BP also called out the racism that African American suffragists had to deal with.

But several items were missing from the monument. BP didn't grapple with the fact that since the United States was in the throes of the Jim Crow laws, white suffragists were forced to walk a wafer-thin line between playing realpolitik and completely succumbing to Southern white supremacists. I discuss that topic in Chapter 2 in the section titled "Racism, White Suffragists, 'Great Men,' and the Double Standard." BP didn't honor Carrie Chapman Catt's superb leadership of the National American Woman Suffrage Association (NAWSA), nor did it emphasize how the magic of Catt's yin and Paul's yang catapulted the movement forward.

It was frustrating to see that the monument only acknowledged what the suffragists did. It didn't really honor them. BP never hinted that suffragists are victims of historical malpractice, whereby history textbooks trivialize their achievement with a "women were given the vote" statement.

When I first heard about BP after President Obama designated it as a national monument in 2016, I didn't expect it to cover Alice Paul's ERA activism in much depth. I thought it was doing a great job by telling us about the National Woman's Party (NWP) Congressional Voting Card Index, a lobbying innovation that gave detailed, sometimes humorous information about all members of Congress, along with their positions on ERA.

But after I read Rebecca DeWolf's *Gendered Citizenship*, I realized that BP could have told many more great stories about the cutting-edge nature of the ERA campaign from 1920 to 1963, including the fraught relationship between Alice Paul and Eleanor Roosevelt.

I also wanted to see more pictures of activists and politicians visiting the house. At an online API presentation a few years ago, I saw pictures of Sen. Kay Bailey Hutchison and Supreme Court Justice Ruth Bader Ginsburg dining at the house and was disappointed that they weren't included in the exhibits.

BP exhibits are somewhat interactive. They ask questions and encourage people to vote and get politically involved. But they need to urge history teachers to adequately cover the Women's Suffrage Movement in their classes. They also need to challenge the public to make sure that the suffragists' great innovations and sacrifices are never forgotten or trivialized.

Despite these limitations, when I went to a coffee that Sen. John Cornyn had for his constituents, I encouraged a staffer who had minored in history to visit BP. It's a three-minute walk from the Hart Building, where Cornyn's office is located. Not surprisingly, the staffer had never heard of Alice Paul. I told him that his history professors hadn't done their job.

When I visited the office of my Congressman, Colin Allred, I also urged the staffers to tour BP, especially since it's across the street from the Supreme Court. Again, I had to educate them about Alice Paul. I told them that even if you don't think the Women's Suffrage Movement is exciting, this is crucial history. If we don't support the monument, some misogynistic politician is going to campaign for reduced funding with the argument that it's a waste of taxpayers' money. Attendance at BP is so low that it's open only on Thursday through Sunday.

When I see how Alice Paul has gotten belittled in places that should honor her, I wonder: *Would you give your whole life to a noble and necessary cause if you knew you were going to get trashed and barely acknowledged one hundred years later?*

Alice Paul made tremendous personal and professional sacrifices to work for women's rights at a time when feminism was a much more taboo word than it is now. She used her inheritance to finance her activist career and didn't get paid for her work. Paul, who loved to dance,[46] could have foxtrotted her way through life and been a conventional super-volunteer who stayed away from women's rights activism. But she willingly chose the harder way—the much, much harder way—a way that most of us would be terrified of contemplating.

Yes, I know I'm in danger of idolizing her. So now I will stay in the honor zone and summarize her flaws and limitations.

As we all know, Paul was not intersectional. Like most social justice activists of her generation, including civil rights activists, she didn't think she needed to examine the systemic privileges and biases she inherited from her culture except for the ones that oppressed her. (Nevertheless, she still had to play realpolitik. Unabashed solidarity with African American women's suffrage organizations probably would have killed the Nineteenth Amendment. A coalition with civil rights groups could have severely weakened the nascent ERA movement. In a sense, Paul had the same dilemma as New Deal Democrats. *They needed Southern votes. Full stop.*)

Paul was not a great public speaker, nor was she a natural at banter and small talk, which is probably why she gave few interviews and didn't appear on radio and TV. Paul was a workaholic. She did not suffer fools gladly and was better suited to leading small, single-issue, cutting-edge groups instead of large, mainstream, multi-issue organizations. She was at her best as a lobbyist, director, strategist, and choreographer.

Neither she nor Carrie Chapman Catt gave each other credit for their accomplishments, and they never admitted how much they needed each other.

In retrospect, one of Paul's biggest mistakes was not writing one detailed autobiography after the Nineteenth Amendment passed and another one towards the end of her life, especially when considering the put-downs she's getting in the year 2025.

"She was a reticent person who didn't see her own story as something that should or could be shared," said Lucienne Beard, former executive director of API.[47]

But she was still one hell of an activist, right up there with the brilliant, heroic, and flawed King, Gandhi, and Mandela. Women and men of all races, classes, religions, and sexualities would be a lot worse off today without Alice Paul. I shudder to think of what could have happened to the Jewish refugees she helped if she hadn't lived in Switzerland during the Nazi era. I also wish ERA advocates had taken her advice when she told them to say "no" to a deadline on passing the amendment.

Even the Alice Paul Center with its warts-and-all philosophy admits that "few individuals have had as much impact on American history as has Alice Paul."[48] She has given us so much. It is time to stop belittling her and treat her with the honor she deserves.

Dropping the Inez Milholland Campaign
for the Presidential Citizens Medal

In 2016, the National Women's History Project (NWHP, now known as the National Women's History Alliance) asked me to sign an online petition to award Inez Milholland the Presidential Citizens Medal, the second highest civilian award in the nation. I not only signed it, I encouraged several friends to stamp their signatures on the petition for the beautiful, charismatic, and forgotten suffrage martyr. Many told me they happily complied. According to Marguerite Kearns, co-chair of the Inez Milholland Centennial, 1,116 people signed the petition.[49]

Both the petition and NWHP lobbying must have had some impact, for California Congresswoman Jackie Speier nominated Milholland for the medal and called her "a shining star in the pantheon of inspiring leaders."[50] Speier did a good job educating her colleagues about Milholland's life. She talked about Milholland's upper-class childhood in New York and London and how much activism she packed into her short life: as a leader of suffrage rallies at Vassar; as "the lady on the white horse" who led the spectacular Suffrage Parade in 1913; and as a pioneering attorney who fought for women's rights, prison reform, abolition of the death penalty, racial justice (she was a charter member of the NAACP), and many other issues.[51]

Speier described Milholland's last, tragic campaign. Even by today's standards, it was a grueling train tour. In the fall of 1916, Milholland toured the western states to persuade women to vote against Woodrow Wilson for president and send a message that Congress would pay a high price for sidelining women's rights:

> Now, for the first time in our history, women have the power to enforce their demands and the weapon with which to fight for woman's liberation ... Liberty must be fought for. And, women of the nation, this is the time to fight.[52]

Speier emphasized that Milholland continued the tour despite deep health problems, and as a result, she became a suffrage martyr:

> In late October, exhausted and overcome by pain, the young suffragist collapsed while demanding liberty on a stage in Los Angeles. A month later, despite repeated blood transfusions, she died of pernicious anemia, having just turned thirty.[53]

Speier noted, "On Christmas Day 1916, the National Woman's Party held an unprecedented memorial for her under the rotunda in Statuary Hall in the national Capitol. She became the first woman to be so honored. A week later, aroused by her sacrifice, suffragists began to picket the White House."[54]

Even with Speier's great promotion, the nomination stayed on President Obama's desk.

It was obvious that if Hillary Rodham Clinton had won the presidential election, the campaign would have continued and Milholland probably would have won the medal. But the new Oval Office occupant was not exactly an exemplar of pro-feminist views, and so the project died. The disgust of Trump's presidency provoked so many of us into marches and on-the-streets activism that campaigning for a Presidential Citizens Medal seemed like a luxury. Besides, the short documentary *Forward Into Light*, with its fantastic footage of activists and suffrage marches, reassured us that the eloquent, photogenic activist, the Gloria Steinem of her day, would not be completely forgotten. Several hundred women even gathered at Milholland's grave in Lewis, New York, for a touching tribute during the global Women's March of 2017. [55]

Nevertheless, a documentary or a tribute will never take the place of a medal. The Presidential Citizens Medal would mean that Inez Milholland has finally arrived. It would mean that, at last, the nation has recognized her for exceptional bravery, service, eloquence, and sacrifice and that she is where she belongs, up there with the "great men of history."

When I was doing research for this book, I found out that, far from being forgotten, Inez Milholland was the star of a photo essay created in 2021 by Dallas-based visual historian Jeanine Michna-Bales. She had developed an exhibit on Milholland's ill-fated western campaign in 1916, and it had made its debut at the Photographs Do Not Bend Gallery in the Dallas Design District. The presentation got good reviews in the *Dallas Morning News*, *Smithsonian Magazine*, and the *New York Times*. I have no idea why I missed it, other than that we were so isolated by the pandemic.

Fortunately, I was able to experience Michna-Bales's exhibit through her lovely coffee-table book, *Standing Together: Inez Milholland's Final Campaign for Women's Suffrage*. By focusing completely on Milholland's western campaign, Michna-Bales described the groundbreaking nature of Milholland's brutal tour and her deep sacrifices much more effectively than *Iron Jawed Angels* and *Suffs*.

The period from 1913 until 1920 is so rich with great suffrage stories that Milholland's campaign often gets squeezed in the shuffle, sandwiched in between the spectacular Suffrage Parade and the riveting White House protests. But Michna-Bales's emphasis on Milholland's tour gave us a day-by-day account through artifacts; newspaper articles; reports of people getting turned away because her performances always sold out; letters to her beloved husband, Eugen Jan Boissevain; beautiful photographs; and dramatizations. Michna-Bales added crucial new details about Milholland. Her health problems started before the tour, and she was not as confident as she appeared in front of cheering, standing-room-only audiences. Before she left New York, "she felt exhausted, her head ached, and her heart sometimes beat oddly." [56]

In March 2025, Michna-Bales started to launch a traveling exhibition of *Standing Together*. I'm excited that the exhibit has the promise of a long shelf life. But Michna-Bales's presentation needs to be accompanied by a campaign for the Presidential Citizens Medal. Otherwise, her show will have the same fate as other suffrage exhibits—historical busywork that doesn't help make Milholland more of a household word. I know we must deal with political authoritarianism. But dropping a campaign for a medal implies that Milholland is not good enough, that she is not worth fighting for. Canceling a campaign gives patriarchy an easy victory.

Ever since 2008, feminists and suffrage historians have campaigned for Alice Paul to get the Congressional Gold Medal, the oldest and highest civilian award in the country. In 2024 the House approved, 412-1, the Alice Paul Women's Suffrage Congressional Gold Medal Act (H.R. 406). [57] The bill failed to get through the Senate. Though Paul didn't make the cut in 2024, several women did win the Congressional Gold Medal that year. Among them were Billie Jean King and the NASA mathematicians, programmers, and engineers featured in *Hidden Figures* (Katherine Johnson, Mary Jackson, Dorothy Vaughan, Christine Darden).

Before he left office, Biden awarded the Presidential Medal of Freedom to nineteen people, only four of them women: Jane

Goodall, Anna Wintour, Fannie Lou Hamer (posthumous), and Hillary Rodham Clinton. However, women won nine out of twenty Presidential Citizens Medals: Liz Cheney, Carolyn McCarthy, Mary L. Bonauto, Nancy Landon Kassebaum, Diane Carlson Evans, Frances M. Visco, Paula S. Wallace, Mitsuye Endo Tsutsumi (posthumous), and Eleanor Smeal. I was pleasantly surprised when Smeal, founder and president of the Feminist Majority Foundation, won an award.

All the women listed above richly deserved those honors, and yet I'm disgusted that suffragists have never gotten posthumous recognition. We all know that Trump is not going to pay attention to the "suffs," but we still need to lay the groundwork for a multitude of great suffragists, including Alice Paul and Inez Milholland, to get the Presidential Medal of Freedom.

Feminists and suffrage historians, this is the time to fight.

Forgetting the Suffragists
Abused by their Families

During the 2016 and 2024 presidential campaigns, there were several intense online discussions about whether conservative husbands were coercing their wives into voting for Trump. The arguments led to articles that asked if most married women vote like their husbands because the hubbies are swaying them or because they have the same political worldview. Marie Solis, a staff writer at *Vice*, concluded from her research, "It may be that women's age, level of education, and socioeconomic circumstance are better indicators of how married women vote than marriage alone." [58]

Alana Valko of *Buzzfeed* took a different approach. She collected a series of responses posted on X (formerly Twitter) to the story of an eighty-one-year-old widow who voted for the first time in her life because her husband had kept her from going to the polls. [59]

Most of the responses were boilerplate: I can't believe this is happening in 2024; stop insulting Republicans; Democrats think conservatives are stuck in the 1950s. But several women and election workers told their own stories, which led many of us to suspect that these abuses are more common than we think. Valko quoted a user named "Anonymous":

> My father. He said, and I quote, "The downfall of this country was when they gave women the right to vote, because women are too stupid to know how to vote." [60]

Since Solis and Valko were writing articles about the suppression of married women voters, I was curious to find out if they said anything about suffragists. Again, they had different takes. Solis made this claim:

> According to Christina Wolbrecht, the co-author of *A Century of Votes for Women*, a camp of early suffragists argued, somewhat counterintuitively, that since women would likely vote the same way as their husbands, they would merely double the vote, rather than dramatically shift the landscape of electoral politics, as some feared. [61]

Counterintuitively? If men had made those arguments, they would have been lauded for clever politicking. Valko quoted a commenter named Chakram-sola, whose great-great-grandmother had been a suffragist:

> My grandmother's grandmother was a suffragette. Her family put her into an asylum for that, where she committed suicide. My grandmother joined the League of Women Voters because of her. She had all boys, and they're also feminists (one of them my dad).

I would love to hear more about Chakram-sola's story and am disappointed that Valko didn't contact her for an interview. She has a

Buzzfeed account, and it probably wouldn't have been too difficult for Valko to write an article.

In conversations with suffrage history advocates, there have been times when someone has brought up an anecdote about, say, a woman whose husband beat her because he found out that she gave some of her allowance to NAWSA. Even though these stories are believable because of the prevalence of domestic violence, they don't get publicized because nobody has provided evidence.

However, whenever a woman claims that an ancestor was committed to an asylum because her husband or father hated her suffrage activism, I don't hear any suffrage historians jumping on the story and encouraging her to write an article or book with documented proof. These stories are crucial to history. They provide another window into nineteenth and early twentieth century family values and give more evidence of the heroism it took for women to claim their voting rights.

Indeed, in the age of Trump and Musk, suffrage skeptics and blatant anti-suffragists have gotten closer to center stage: Peter Thiel, Ann Coulter, and Abby Johnson, who wants to bring back "household voting"; Pastor Joel Webbon, who whined that the Nineteenth Amendment stole half of his household vote; and several others. [62]

We cannot afford to dismiss these patriarchalists as harmless crackpots anymore. Again, don't forget suffragists abused by their husbands. And don't ignore twenty-first century women coerced by their husbands at the polls.

Lauding Harry Burn While Ignoring Joseph Hanover

One of the most popular suffrage stories is Harry Burn's last-minute "Aye" vote in the Tennessee state House, a stance that broke the gridlock on the Nineteenth Amendment and enabled it to become the law of the land. Burn, a Republican congressman, was an "anti" until his mother, Febb Ensminger Burn, wrote him a note proclaiming how much she hated an anti-suffrage speech and admonishing him to "respect Mrs. Catt" and say yes to votes for women.

Burn got considerable flak for changing his stance, but he still got narrowly reelected. When asked why he switched sides, he always disarmed audiences with, "I knew that a mother's advice is always safest for a boy to follow, and my mother wanted me to vote for ratification." [63]

Hollywood couldn't have done it any better. However, there is a Tennessee suffrage story that has even more drama than the Harry Burn chronicle, but it has no traction with the public. Joseph Hanover was born in Poland to Orthodox Jewish parents. He and his family fled the Russian pogroms when he was a child, and they eventually settled in Memphis. After his parents happily became American citizens, he asked, "Why can't Mother vote?" He never got a convincing answer.

Hanover worked at his father's dry goods store, attended night school, and became a lawyer. In 1918, he was elected to the Tennessee House of Representatives as an independent. His reason for getting into politics was to help ensure that the Nineteenth Amendment would get into the Constitution. Yes, you heard it right. He went into politics so that he could help make the Nineteenth Amendment happen. His chance to help make that dream come true came two years later.

When Carrie Chapman Catt came to Tennessee and evaluated the suffrage scene, she noticed a legislator with tremendous knowledge and conviction about women's suffrage coupled with exceptional political skills. She summoned Joe Hanover to her suite at the Hermitage Hotel, where she bluntly told him that the suffs were losing the battle and that she wanted him to lead the legislative fight.

Hanover was surprised by her request. As an independent Jewish city boy in a legislature overwhelmingly controlled by rural Protestant Democrats, what difference could he make? Again, showing her great political instincts, Catt knew that no Tennessee legislator was more committed to women's suffrage than Joe Hanover and that, as an independent, he was respected on both sides of the aisle. Hanover, as one of the few lawyers in the legislature, had a reputation for writing good pieces of legislation. Both Democrats and Republicans said that if you want a bill or resolution done right, ask Joe to do it.

He said yes to Catt's request, but in the words of Hanover biographer Bill Haltom, it almost cost him his life:

> When the word got out that Joe Hanover was going to lead the fight for the ratification of the Nineteenth Amendment, that evening, when he was in the elevator at the Hermitage Hotel, he was attacked by two men. One called him a kike, the other called him a Bolshevik. [64]

Hanover survived the attack, but the governor of Tennessee insisted on a bodyguard. Throughout the legislative session, the bodyguard was always with him. The suffrage fight was so stressful that Hanover lost weight, got an ulcer, and suffered from insomnia. His phone was always ringing. Sometimes, men threatened him. At other times, women who claimed to be suffragists offered to come to his room to help him. He never fell for that honey trap.

Hanover corralled the pro-suffrage politicians and managed to keep them together despite bribes from railroad, manufacturing, and liquor lobbyists. Like Carrie Chapman Catt, he was a smooth operator:

> When a longtime ally told him, "Sorry, Joe, but I'm going to have to leave you suffrage boys. The antis just paid me three hundred dollars," Hanover hadn't flinched. "Well, you're a pretty cheap vote," he'd said, "I hear they're paying the others a thousand." Enraged, the man switched his vote back and said this time he wouldn't budge. [65]

Because of Joe Hanover, Harry Burn's vote made a difference. Thanks to the advocacy of Tennessee suffrage historians, he is finally starting to get the recognition he deserves. Bill Haltom's *Why Can't Mother Vote? Joseph Hanover and the Unfinished Business of Democracy* has gotten superb reviews, and Hanover was honored on the Equality Trailblazers: Memphis Suffrage Monument. But he was ignored in *Suffs, The Vote,* and the Turning Point Suffragist Memorial in Virginia. There is no suffrage cocktail at the Hermitage named after "Mr. Joe," but the hotel bar has cocktails named after other Tennessee suffrage icons. Still, Hanover's story is so compelling that if we keep publicizing him, he will probably become as famous as Harry Burn.

I hope the Hanover story will compel more historians and journalists to respect the fact that suffragists and their male allies were often in harm's way and had to deal with considerable violence. I also hope it compels them to treat the Women's Suffrage Movement's philosophy of nonviolent resistance with the respect it deserves.

Before I went to Austin for the Women's March of 2017, I read several Facebook comments on the fine art of organizing protests. One of the most striking was an advertisement for a class on nonviolent protest techniques. The leaders said they were going to focus on Martin Luther King's principles. They said nothing about the philosophy of nonviolence in the Women's Suffrage Movement or about the fact that several activists were Quakers.

I fear that as Hanover's story becomes better known, it will overshadow the great work of the women who led the Tennessee suffrage movement. I have heard Tennessee women laud him as a great hero while taking for granted the heroism of Carrie Chapman Catt, Sue Shelton White, Anne Dallas Dudley, Juno Frankie Pierce, Mattie Coleman, and several other women.

Several years ago, I attended a church that prided itself on inclusiveness. When I suggested to the senior pastor that she pay homage to the Seneca Falls pioneers in a July sermon, she complied. However, she quoted Frederick Douglass extensively and took the women leaders for granted. When I complained, she grudgingly admitted that she should have given more credit to Elizabeth Cady Stanton. After she moved to another church and a young male pastor took her place, I suggested that he honor the Seneca Falls activists during a church service in July. He complied and made the same mistake. He treated Frederick Douglass like Superman and acted like Elizabeth Cady Stanton and Lucretia Mott were bit players. When I complained, he stonewalled.

When we honor Joseph Hanover, it is imperative that we also laud Carrie Chapman Catt's great field marshal work. She was the only person who saw the difference Hanover could make. The next time someone tells the Harry Burn story, we need to insist that they also laud Carrie Chapman Catt and Joseph Hanover. It deserves to become the stuff of legends.

Don't Mess with Texas Women—
Unless They're Imprisoned Suffragists

When I was updating the National Votes for Women Trail database with Texas suffrage sites in 2018, I started wondering if any Lone Star suffragists went to prison. After a basic Google search, I was pleasantly surprised to find that two Texans protested with Alice Paul and were incarcerated: Lucille Shields of Amarillo and Elizabeth Kalb of Houston. Not only that, but I was stunned to find that Texas had a state chapter of the National Woman's Party, led by Clara Snell Wolfe of Austin.

You heard it right—an NWP chapter in Texas. Now I know it was based in Austin, that liberal island in an ocean full of conservatives,[66] but still, NWP and Texas don't seem like a natural match. Nevertheless, Alice Paul and Lucy Burns campaigned in the Alamo State, and San Antonio and El Paso were stops on the Prison Special. Then, as now, activists couldn't ignore Texas if they wanted to get a federal law passed.

After I discovered these exciting facts, I started working with Texas members of the National Collaborative for Women's History Sites to see if we could get National Votes for Women Trail markers for these heroic activists. We didn't have any luck with Lucille Shields, one of the first NWP activists to go to prison. There were no remnants of her

Photo by Joanne M. Callahan

Figure 1: Tribute to Lucille Shields, Turning Point Suffragist Memorial at Occoquan Park in Lorton, Virginia.

life in Amarillo—no dwelling where she lived, no buildings or parks where she did activism, no workplace . . . not even a grave site, because she died in Miami in 1968. All we have is a small tribute to her at the Turning Point Suffragist Memorial in Virginia and a great quote.

"In jail . . . you realize more keenly the years that women have struggled to be free and the tasks that they have been forced to leave undone for lack of power to do them."[67]

Concerning Elizabeth Kalb, we found that her birth name was Hildegard Elizabeth Kalb and that she was born in Ohio and moved with her family to a farm in the Houston area when she was thirteen. She attended Rice Institute (now Rice University) and participated in the Watchfire demonstrations.[68] She was arrested, spent five days in prison, and was released in an ambulance because she got the 1918 flu (the "Spanish" flu). Fresh with the memory of Inez Milholland, authorities feared the impact of another suffrage martyr, which prompted a Rice alumna to quip that Kalb was probably the first Rice graduate who went to jail.[69] In typical Texas fashion, the farm where she spent her teenage years is now a suburb. It would have been wonderful to dedicate a National Votes for Women Trail marker to her at Rice, but since none of us had any connections or clout at the "Ivy of the South," we gave up.

At first, Clara Snell Wolfe looked promising. For a while, it seemed like the Illinois native was a shoo-in for a National Votes for Women Trail marker. Wolfe had fought for a federal suffrage amendment in "states rights" Texas, participated in the White House protests, and defended them in Texas newspapers. The house she shared with her husband, an economics professor at UT Austin, still exists. We contacted the owner, who said she admired Wolfe because "those were the days when protesting was a much, much bigger risk than it is now." However, when the owner saw the sign, she thought it was too big and sadly declined.[70] Getting a historical marker is a chancy business, and it's a lot harder than most people realize.

I had given up on getting National Votes for Women Trail markers for these Texas NWP activists but continued to promote them at every opportunity. It was usually hope and promise followed by disappointment. A Texas company that promotes conservation and heritage tourism expressed interest in building interpretative panels for Texas suffragists, including Clara Snell Wolfe. But nothing came of it at the time. Perhaps at some point in the future, the right people will step forward to sponsor building those interpretative panels.

In the midst of so many setbacks, I did have one success story. In 2020, when I heard about the women's suffrage exhibit at the Bullock Texas State History Museum, I called and asked the curator if she had included information about Lucille Shields, Elizabeth Kalb, and Clara Snell Wolfe. She wasn't familiar with them, but she promised to do more research.[71] Several months later, I perused the Bullock website and was pleasantly surprised to see a section that described the NWP and mentioned Kalb's and Shields's heroism. It even included an artifact of Doris Stevens's *Jailed for Freedom* from the Rice University archives, which Elizabeth Kalb autographed and dedicated "to the girls of Rice past and present." [72]

After seeing that the Bullock Museum leaders could act like the adults in the room around the Texas NWP, I was losing my patience with Texas historians who acted like they didn't exist. Both Alice Paul and the Texas NWP were ignored in an August 2020 *Texas Observer* article on the Women's Suffrage Movement. [73] Of course, I wrote an angry protest letter. [74] While *Citizens at Last*, the fine documentary on the Texas suffrage movement, did mention Alice Paul, it erased Clara Snell Wolfe, Lucille Shields, and Elizabeth Kalb. I wasn't shy about voicing my disagreement in the Contact Us section of the website. [75] There was no excuse to ignore them.

If historians think that Clara Snell Wolfe had no impact on the Texas suffrage movement, they need to tell us why and give convincing evidence. They also need to answer these questions: Why did Alice Paul and Lucy Burns campaign in the state? Why was San Antonio a stop on the Prison Special? Why did the women on the Prison Special stage an impromptu suffrage rally at the El Paso train station when the train had technical difficulties, and they had to stop for the night? If the NWP was useless in the Lone Star State, they may as well have taken a break and ventured off to a Mexican restaurant, a novelty for most Americans in 1919. Even if the Texas NWP was so incompatible with the culture that it couldn't have any impact, Texas suffrage historians still need to honor the heroism of Lucille Shields and Elizabeth Kalb.

When I visited the Belmont-Paul monument in 2024, I discovered Shirley M. Marshall's *A Radical Suffragist in Washington, D.C.: An Inside Story of the National Woman's Party* in the gift shop and was pleasantly surprised to find that the book was about Elizabeth Kalb. Since I had been disappointed so many times, I held back my excitement but still hoped that the book would raise the stature of imprisoned Texas suffragists.

Marshall was in a unique position to write about Kalb. They met when Marshall was a child in Virginia. Her parents were friends with Kalb and her husband, Edward Smith Handy. After Kalb died,

Marshall's father inherited her papers and those of her husband. In that stash were several letters that Kalb wrote to her mother from September 13, 1918, when Kalb arrived in Washington, DC, to volunteer with the NWP, until January 20, 1919, when her mother came to DC to do activism with her.

A Radical Suffragist starts out by briefly describing the history of the Women's Suffrage Movement. Marshall then displays the letters that Kalb wrote to her mother, with very little editing. We don't see the letters that her mother wrote in return. She briefly describes Kalb's life after the Nineteenth Amendment was ratified. Marshall has a great picture of Kalb with her mother and grandmother in "Three Generations of Suffragists," a 1921 article in the *Baltimore Sun*.[76] She writes a few good "I didn't know whether to laugh or cry" paragraphs about the fact that many imprisoned suffragists couldn't vote because they lived in Washington, DC. Marshall guesses that Kalb may have voted in Texas or Ohio, because "if her parents still owned property in Texas, she might have used that state for residency or she might have used her father's address in Ohio."[77]

But the book spirals downhill in the last three chapters: "Who's Missing," an exposé of racism in the movement; "Limits of an Eyewitness," a list of systemic privileges that Kalb enjoyed; and "Other Viewpoints," a profile of suffragists who don't fit the affluent white Anglo-Saxon Protestant stereotype.

Unfortunately, her discussion of racism in the suffrage movement is chronicled in such broad brushstrokes that it degenerates into a hatchet job. Sorry, but in the age of Jim Crow, NAWSA and the NWP were forced to play realpolitik. Whether they did it well or poorly is up for debate, but as historian Judith McArthur explains, "If all thirteen Southern states had stood together and refused to ratify [the women's suffrage amendment], *as the governor of Louisiana was urging*, NAWSA [and the NWP] couldn't possibly have gotten the necessary thirty-six votes."[78]

Marshall notes the problems with "history lessons focusing on heroes as mythically perfect people that led the fight for justice."[79] But she doesn't admit that those heroes are almost always men, that they always get a pass on their sexism/misogyny, and that no suffragist or historical feminist has ever been admitted to that pantheon. Indeed, Marshall never calls Kalb and other imprisoned suffragists heroic, and she acts like Kalb's work for the NWP, first as a volunteer and later as an employee, was a fun, youthful, time-of-her-life adventure.[80]

Her "Limits of an Eyewitness" chapter is even more insulting to Elizabeth Kalb. She calls Kalb's letters an eyewitness account, which implies that Kalb was just an observer.

Marshall pounds on the fact that "she brought a viewpoint shaped by privilege"—race, class, family support, income, political access.[81] She even points a finger at the "privilege" of Kalb's mother, who ran a stenography business. Considering that in 1919, only 5 percent to 12 percent of married women were in the labor force, I would congratulate Benigna Green Kalb on that pioneering.[82] But I would also wonder if her husband's peach farm was having problems, which forced her to start a business.

When Elizabeth Kalb was arrested, her mother telegrammed Sen. Morris Sheppard of Texas, a suffrage supporter, and asked him to visit the jail. Even though he ignored that request, he responded to Benigna and asked the superintendent of police for a report on prison conditions.[83] I agree with Marshall that Sheppard answered Benigna Kalb because of her race and class privilege. But there is more to the story than privilege: A mother's love and anguish for her daughter, activist solidarity, and a politician providing some level of constituent service.

Marshall doesn't mention that Kalb is a German name. So is Hildegard. She notes that Elizabeth Kalb dropped the Hildegard from her name when she began college and started calling herself Elizabeth Green in 1922 but doesn't tell us why.[84] Considering the sudden, deep discrimination against Americans of German descent during WWI and shortly thereafter, I wouldn't be surprised if it played a role in her name change. But Marshall, so attuned to issues of privilege and the lack thereof, never gives us an answer. She notes that Elizabeth Kalb advocated for Native American water rights in California and reported on China's civil war, but unfortunately, she doesn't elaborate on it. [85]

In the age of Trump, when Texas routinely gets on "worst states for women" lists, it's hard to believe that in the recent past, people were asking, "What do they put in the water?" because the state had so many powerful women. Judge Sarah Hughes, Ambassador Anne Legendre Armstrong, restaurateur Ninfa Rodriguez Laurenzo, rock star Janis Joplin, Congresswoman Barbara Jordan, Sen. Kay Bailey Hutchison, Gov. Ann Richards, political humorist Molly Ivins, abortion rights attorney Sarah Weddington, and so many others . . . all of them put substance behind the cliché, "Don't mess with Texas women."

Since she had lived in Ohio, Texas, Illinois, Washington, DC, California, Virginia, China, and likely many more places throughout her life, Kalb probably didn't consider herself a Texan. But this statement of hers, with its can-do spirit, is as Texas as it gets:

> So long as people said "Please" too long and too meekly, they never got anything, but when they grew earnest enough and well-informed enough and said, "We Demand . . ."—they actually got what they demanded—after, of course, careful organization, detailed and widespread propaganda, far-visioned planning, refusal to be discouraged . . . [86]

And, I would add, the willingness to make the ultimate sacrifice.

Someday, when we finally get a suffrage statue at the Texas state capital, I know that Minnie Fisher Cunningham, Jane Yelvington McCallum, and Annette Finnigan will be honored; that Carrie Chapman Catt will be included because she was such a great mentor and strategist; and that Christia Adair, Maud Sampson Williams, and Jovita Idar will not be erased or sidelined.

If Clara Snell Wolfe, Lucille Shields, and Elizabeth Kalb are excluded from that statue, we will not take it sitting down. There will be pickets. Wolfe, Shields, and Kalb paid more than their dues to the movement, and they did it as Texans.

Don't mess with the Texas NWP.

When Will the World
Finally *Get It* About Lucy Burns?

In September 2024, I visited the Lucy Burns Museum, named after the NWP co-founder who spent more time in jail than any other suffragist in America.

One of Burns's most brutal prison experiences occurred at the Occoquan Workhouse on November 14, 1917. On what became known as the Night of Terror, guards brutally attacked Burns and other suffragists who had been arrested for protests at the White House.

> Burns was beaten and bloodied, gasping for air, and handcuffed with her hands above her head to her cell door. She was forced to stand in the same position for the entire evening. At some point, she was stripped of her clothing, given only a blanket, and remained shackled in that same position in her cell.[87]

Nestled on the former site of the Occoquan Workhouse in rural Lorton, Virginia, the Lucy Burns Museum seems like it is in the middle of nowhere, giving me a sense of what it was like to get arrested in the early twentieth century and disappear into a countryside prison, even a prison that had a reputation for being humane.

The Lucy Burns Museum doesn't have much real estate, but it uses its small space well, working with walls, exhibit boards, a film, and even the floor and the remnants of the prison itself to tell the story of the American Women's Suffrage Movement and Lucy Burns's outstanding contributions. Because the museum is surrounded completely by glass

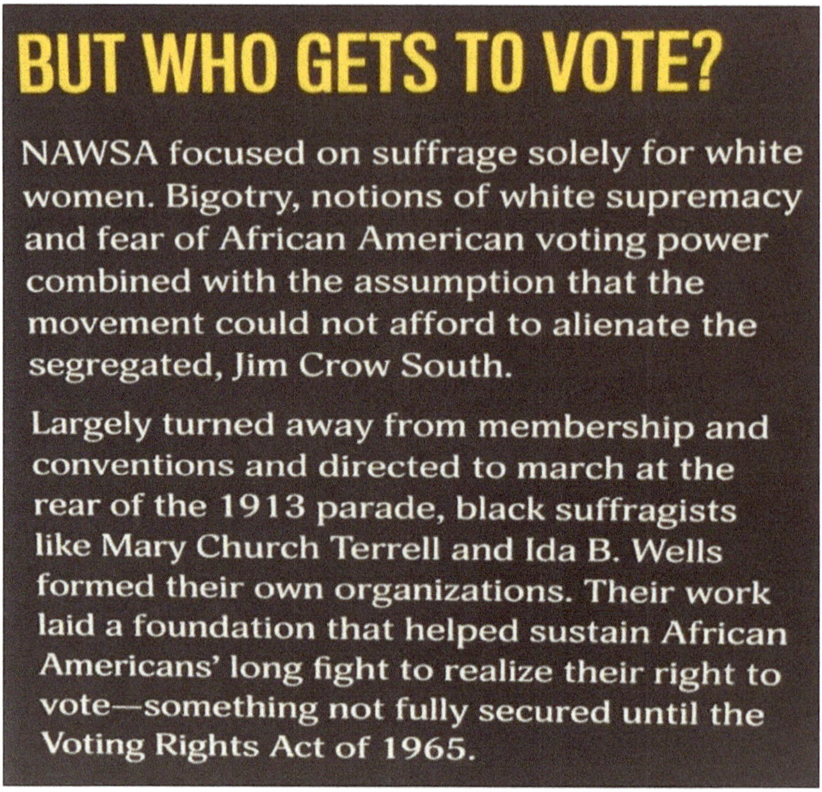

BUT WHO GETS TO VOTE?

NAWSA focused on suffrage solely for white women. Bigotry, notions of white supremacy and fear of African American voting power combined with the assumption that the movement could not afford to alienate the segregated, Jim Crow South.

Largely turned away from membership and conventions and directed to march at the rear of the 1913 parade, black suffragists like Mary Church Terrell and Ida B. Wells formed their own organizations. Their work laid a foundation that helped sustain African Americans' long fight to realize their right to vote—something not fully secured until the Voting Rights Act of 1965.

Photo by Joanne M. Callahan

Figure 2: Exhibit board on racism and the Women's Suffrage Movement at the Lucy Burns Museum.

on one side, there are no problems with lighting on an overcast day.

However, the museum takes a few cheap shots. When I saw the exhibit board on this page, I couldn't help but think, "Here we go again. The beatings will continue . . . "

Sorry, but the issue is a lot more complicated than the rant above, as I explain in my section titled "Racism, White Suffragists, 'Great Men,' and the Double Standard."

Not to be outdone, the museum beat suffragists again in the exhibit pictured on the next page.

The 19th Amendment guaranteed women across the United States the right to vote.

It did not secure voting rights for:

American Indians

Asian Americans

Residents of the District of Columbia

Residents of US Territories

African American men or women

African American men won the right to vote with the 15th Amendment, passed in 1870 during Reconstruction. The 19th Amendment expanded the vote to African American women—on paper. In reality, Jim Crow—a system of state laws and discrimination including poll taxes, literacy tests, economic intimidation and brutal violence—kept black voters from the polls.

The Voting Rights Act of 1965 targeted these barriers and prohibits racial discrimination in voting. The fight to enforce the law and make its promise real continues.

Photo by Joanne M. Callahan

Figure 3: Exhibit board on voting rights issues after the Nineteenth Amendment was ratified—Lucy Burns Museum.

I couldn't help but wonder, "Are they trying to state facts or do they want to bang suffragists' heads against the wall?"

Did they really expect the Nineteenth Amendment to solve every single voting issue in this country?

After showing the brutal fight to get women's voting rights into the Constitution, the exhibit board displayed an astonishing lack of sensitivity. I doubt that they would treat men as badly.

Karen M. Kedrowski, director of the Carrie Chapman Catt Center for Women and Politics, made pretty much the same comments as the author of the exhibit in Figure 3, but with much more finesse and a lot less finger-pointing:

> The story of expanding voting rights in the US is tortured, to our collective shame.
>
> In fact, every extension of voting rights had its limits. The Fifteenth Amendment did not enfranchise formerly enslaved women or other people of color. The Nineteenth Amendment's reach was constrained by racist, restrictive federal and state voting and citizenship laws.
>
> The Voting Rights Act and the Twenty-Sixth Amendment do not address felon voting rights, and the Twenty-Third Amendment failed to provide presidential suffrage to Americans living in US territories.
>
> Nonetheless, these are all important milestones as we march forward to create a more perfect union. Collectively, we must continue this march. [88]

When I started touring the Lucy Burns Museum, I thought I would learn more about her life. But the museum gave a basic biography and didn't really honor her. I got no deep insight into her background, personality, and motivation for retiring from activism after the Nineteenth Amendment passed. At the very least, the museum should have had a separate film about Lucy Burns.

If the museum ever develops that film, it should emphasize Burns's Irish Catholic background. She also had English and Scottish ancestry. As far as I know, no Catholic suffragist has ever gotten excommunicated, even though the church was against women voting. But it was still a significant social risk for the devout Burns to be an outspoken women's rights activist, even if her family was supportive.

The film should also mention that Burns got annoyed because so many people, especially those of the male persuasion, felt free to touch her red hair.

The film should highlight that she was much more than Alice Paul's sidekick. The gregarious and diplomatic Lucy Burns was the type of leader who did whatever it took to keep an organization going, from coordinating protest marches to sweeping the floor. She was a great trouper and had pinch-hit at every job at the NWP. [89]

The film should talk about how she experienced major family tragedies during her activist years. In 1914, her sixty-one-year-old father, Edward, died suddenly of a heart attack at the American Exchange National Bank, where he was the vice president and director. Her mother, Anne, had died two years earlier. [90] High-risk activism took a huge health toll on Burns:

> She lost thirty pounds during the protests. Plagued by not only weight loss, she had bruises and sores on her wrists from her manacling and handcuffing that needed to heal, and she suggested the harsh treatment had affected her heart. [91]

Pundits give two reasons for Burns's retirement from activism after the Nineteenth Amendment passed.

Some say she wanted to move on. Others maintain that she was bitter that so many women, especially the married ones, were passive and apolitical about their rights.

What they neglect to say is that Burns—who had taught English at Erasmus High School in Brooklyn and had taken graduate-level courses at the universities of Bonn, Berlin, and Oxford before she became a suffragist—had a hard time finding a teaching job in 1919. [92]

Burns also had family issues to navigate. Her sister, Janet, had married in 1922 and died tragically in 1923, leaving behind a one-month-old baby. Kelly Marino notes that:

> Sorrow and the culture of death that surrounded her family must have taken a toll on Burns's spirit and energy. Possibly feeling indebted to her sister for support during her suffrage years, Burns chose to help raise her niece . . . [93]

When talking about Burns's supposed bitterness towards passive married women, pundits usually refer to these words from Alice Paul:

> A great many members—for instance, Lucy Burns— she just said, "I don't want to do anything more, I don't want to be on any board or any committee . . . because I think we have done all this for women and we have sacrificed everything we possessed for them . . . let them fight for it now. I am not going to fight for these married women anymore." [94]

When I heard those words, I shouted, "Damn right, Lucy. We need to tell the world that feminist activism is not a free, endlessly renewable resource. It's about time that we honor our heroic suffragists and feminists as much as the Civil Rights Movement honors its icons and as much as the military honors its heroic fighters."

Far from being stereotypically bitter, personal acquaintances said that "she was always a kind and likable person with a delightful personality, despite health struggles as she aged."[95]

So when will people finally *get it* about the mystery of Lucy Burns?

It will happen when they finally admit that heroic suffragists have a right to be honored, not merely acknowledged, and that we can't dump the good fight on other women and expect them to keep sacrificing without recognition and strong support from many women and men.

Alice Paul, Inez Milholland, Lucille Shields, Elizabeth Kalb, Clara Snell Wolfe, and Lucy Burns have not gotten the honor they deserve because they are women who did feminist activism. We must insist on the same level of honor for these women as we give to "great men."

To paraphrase what the priests and sisters taught me so many decades before I learned about imprisoned suffragists, "Greater love has no woman than this: that a woman lay down her life for her friends."

The Protest March
I Wanted to Start at Central Park

In late September 2021, I flew from Dallas to New York primarily to see the Women's Rights Pioneers Monument, a tremendous achievement for the advocacy group Monumental Women. Even though I wore an N95 mask, it felt liberating to travel after several months of feeling like I was in a cloister. Thanks to the COVID vaccine, I could start enjoying life again. I had a great time taking pictures of Meredith Bergmann's compelling statue in beautiful Central Park and felt fortunate to enjoy such sunny autumn weather.

However, I was shocked and offended by so many statements in the description next to the women's rights statue, especially in comparison to the overblown description—basically, HE'S A GENIUS AND SUCH A GREAT HERO!!!!!—next to the Robert Burns statue. I felt like grabbing a bullhorn and starting a protest march. (See Figure 4 and

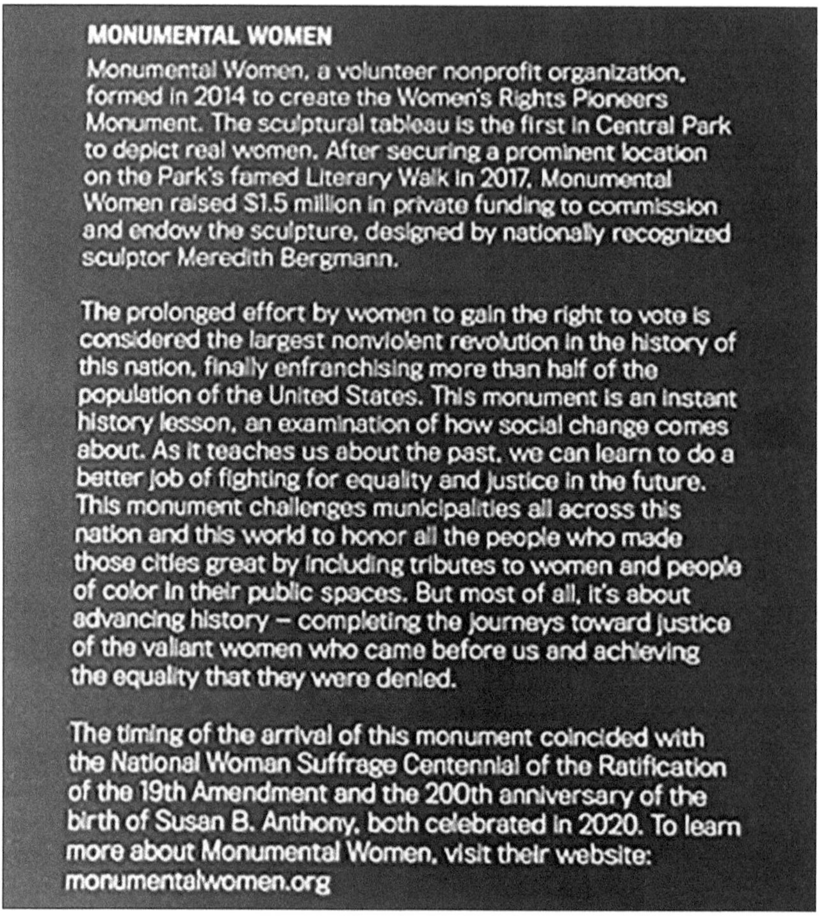

MONUMENTAL WOMEN

Monumental Women, a volunteer nonprofit organization, formed in 2014 to create the Women's Rights Pioneers Monument. The sculptural tableau is the first in Central Park to depict real women. After securing a prominent location on the Park's famed Literary Walk in 2017, Monumental Women raised $1.5 million in private funding to commission and endow the sculpture, designed by nationally recognized sculptor Meredith Bergmann.

The prolonged effort by women to gain the right to vote is considered the largest nonviolent revolution in the history of this nation, finally enfranchising more than half of the population of the United States. This monument is an instant history lesson, an examination of how social change comes about. As it teaches us about the past, we can learn to do a better job of fighting for equality and justice in the future. This monument challenges municipalities all across this nation and this world to honor all the people who made those cities great by including tributes to women and people of color in their public spaces. But most of all, it's about advancing history – completing the journeys toward justice of the valiant women who came before us and achieving the equality that they were denied.

The timing of the arrival of this monument coincided with the National Woman Suffrage Centennial of the Ratification of the 19th Amendment and the 200th anniversary of the birth of Susan B. Anthony, both celebrated in 2020. To learn more about Monumental Women, visit their website: monumentalwomen.org

Photo by Joanne M. Callahan

Figure 4: Description next to the Women's Rights Pioneers Monument.

Figure 5.) So what was so @#$%%^ offensive about the description?

For starters, it said nothing about the genius—yes, the genius—of Elizabeth Cady Stanton, Susan B. Anthony, and Sojourner Truth. The description acted like they were ordinary. Stanton, Anthony, and Truth were the best in the business, and they brought their own unique gifts to the movement: Stanton the visionary philosopher, Anthony the tireless organizer, Truth the prophetic preacher.

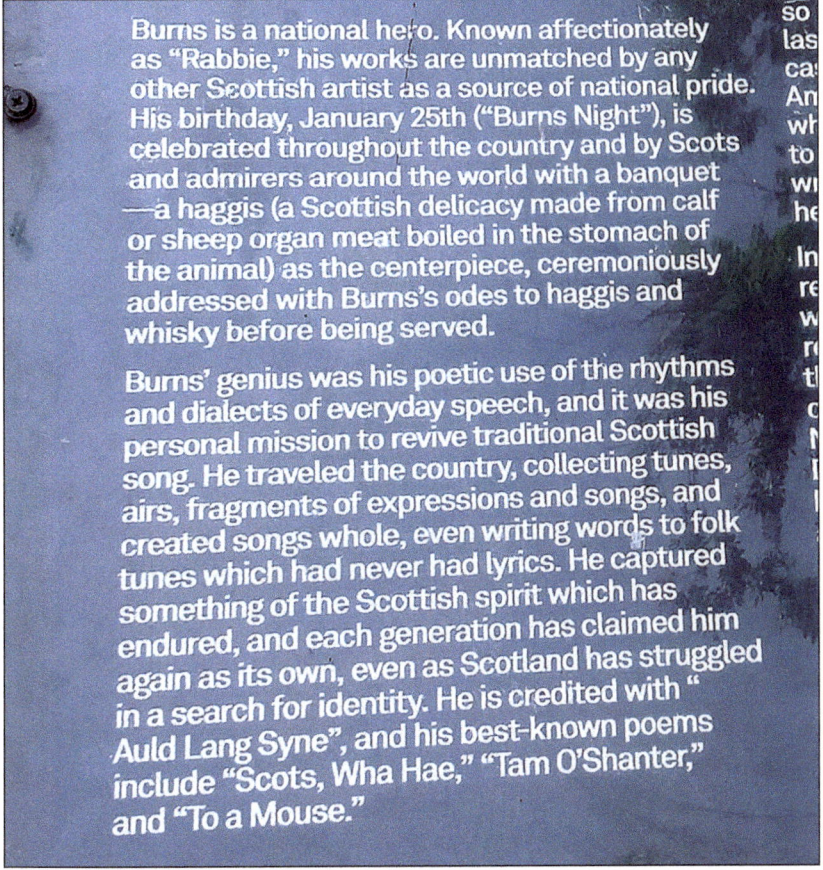

Burns is a national hero. Known affectionately as "Rabbie," his works are unmatched by any other Scottish artist as a source of national pride. His birthday, January 25th ("Burns Night"), is celebrated throughout the country and by Scots and admirers around the world with a banquet —a haggis (a Scottish delicacy made from calf or sheep organ meat boiled in the stomach of the animal) as the centerpiece, ceremoniously addressed with Burns's odes to haggis and whisky before being served.

Burns' genius was his poetic use of the rhythms and dialects of everyday speech, and it was his personal mission to revive traditional Scottish song. He traveled the country, collecting tunes, airs, fragments of expressions and songs, and created songs whole, even writing words to folk tunes which had never had lyrics. He captured something of the Scottish spirit which has endured, and each generation has claimed him again as its own, even as Scotland has struggled in a search for identity. He is credited with "Auld Lang Syne", and his best-known poems include "Scots, Wha Hae," "Tam O'Shanter," and "To a Mouse."

Photo by Jay Dobkin/Wikimedia Commons

Figure 5: Part of an exhibit board next to the Robert Burns statue in Central Park refers to the poet in effusive terms, calling him a "national hero" and describing his "genius."

The description never said that these activists were chosen because they were New Yorkers. It should have shown some regional pride and said that Gotham was an epicenter of the nineteenth century women's rights movement. I felt uncomfortable with the phrase "nonviolent revolution." It reminded me of this pithy statement in Allan G. Johnson's May 8, 2015, *CounterPunch* article, "The Myth of Peaceful Protest":

> The unspoken rule is that power and privilege will respect the people's right to peacefully express their grievances, so long as the people respect the right of power and privilege to ignore them and do nothing at all, as with children being allowed to have their say before the grownups tell them how it's going to be.

The description next to the statue should have summarized the violence that several suffragists endured and should have honored the Women's Suffrage Movement as a great model of nonviolent activism. The description should have said point-blank that Alice Paul and the Silent Sentinels deserve as much recognition for nonviolence as Mahatma Gandhi, Martin Luther King, Daniel and Philip Berrigan, Dorothy Day, and several other activists. The description should have noted that suffragists did not write lengthy treatises, and they didn't coin new words to describe their practice of nonviolent resistance. They just did it.

The following statement was so over the top that I felt like making a huge picket sign, placing it on top of the description, grabbing a bullhorn, and starting a protest march: "As it teaches us about the past, we can learn to do a better job of fighting for equality and justice in the future."

I have seen numerous monuments to male artists, athletes, scientists, military figures, political leaders, and civil rights activists, and I have NEVER seen a statement that even came close to that insult. It is not a tradition to hint at the flaws of "great men" of any race when you build monuments to them. Even the statues of great women artists and scientists do not have insulting comments.

I know that the offensive statement may have been written because several people were hurt during the initial phases of the Women's Suffrage Pioneers project. Unfortunately, only Elizabeth Cady Stanton and Susan B. Anthony were in the statue. I am aware of the activism it took to correct that mistake, and I understand the importance of intersectionality. But there is nothing intersectional about perpetuating the double standard of history, whereby women are expected to be perfect (and never play realpolitik) but we excuse the misogyny of male social justice activists.

When I came home to Dallas, I showed the description to feminist friends, and they had second thoughts about visiting the statue.

I emailed Monumental Women twice and never got an answer. They also didn't return my phone calls. In my letter, I asked, "Who wrote the description? Was it someone from the Parks Department or was it someone from the Central Park Conservancy?"

On August 7, 2022, I sent an email to the Central Park Conservancy and got this response on September 22, 2022, from someone named Matt:

> Thank you so much for taking the time to reach out to us. We always appreciate the public's input. We have passed along your comments to the director of art and antiquities at the Department of Parks and Recreation, who will take them into consideration.
>
> The monument was sponsored and commissioned by Monumental Women (https://monumentalwomen. org/), who authored the sign.
>
> The sign is temporary and will ultimately be replaced by a Parks Department sign.

I responded to Matt and asked for his phone number because I had questions about his comments and wanted him to clarify them. I never got an answer. I suspected the conservancy was placating me.

When I went back to New York in 2024 to see *Suffs*, I spent an afternoon at Central Park and saw the statue and the description. Nothing had changed. Absolutely nothing. However, I still receive fundraising emails from Monumental Women.

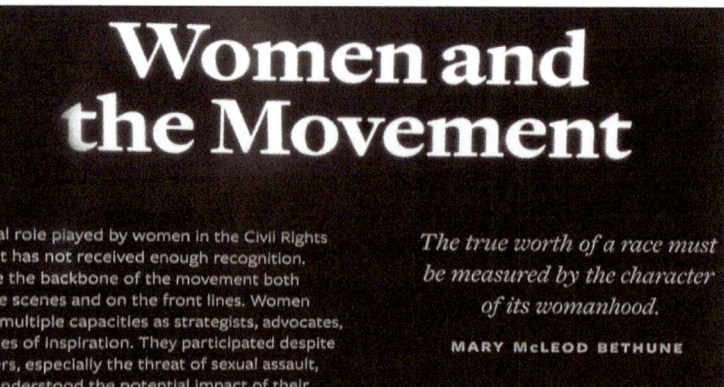

Women and the Movement

The critical role played by women in the Civil Rights Movement has not received enough recognition. They were the backbone of the movement both behind the scenes and on the front lines. Women served in multiple capacities as strategists, advocates, and sources of inspiration. They participated despite the dangers, especially the threat of sexual assault, for they understood the potential impact of their actions for future generations.

The true worth of a race must be measured by the character of its womanhood.

MARY McLEOD BETHUNE

Photo by Joanne M. Callahan

Figure 6: Women and the Movement exhibit board at the National Museum of African American History and Culture.

If We Really Want to Honor Black, Latina, and Asian and Native American Suffragists

At the end of my tour of the extraordinary National Museum of African American History and Culture in September 2024, I saw the exhibit board in Figure 6 above.

Some viewers may think that the board honored women, especially after enjoying the museum's stunning architecture, beautiful gardens, excellent cafeteria, and superb state-of-the-art multimedia presentations, but I thought it was patronizing. When I hear someone say, "Women were the backbone," I think, "Oh my God, they did all the essential but thankless housework, childcare, and emotional labor, and then they did the tedious but oh-so-necessary administrative work. Meanwhile, the men got all the glory as heroes and geniuses."

The board never said that the women's contributions were innovative, brilliant, or outstanding; it never lauded their heroism; and it was silent about the deep sexism and misogyny they encountered in both the Civil Rights Movement and the general culture.

Indeed, there was a subtle condescension in the Ida B. Wells exhibits in the museum. The exhibits say that Wells was an anti-lynching activist, but they never lauded her as a *pioneer* in that work. The museum should have taken the same approach as the *Guardian*:

> Wells was galvanized to count, investigate, and report lynchings in America **as no one had done before**, hurling her five-foot frame into hostile territory with all the fearlessness of a war reporter . . .
>
> She was **a trailblazer in every way** . . . as a feminist, as a suffragist, as an investigative reporter, as a civil rights leader. She was just an all-around badass.
>
> In 1894, she published a pamphlet, the *Red Record*, **the first statistical report** of the history of American lynchings, a **forerunner** of data journalism . . . [96]

The museum was far from understated about the achievements of Frederick Douglass, W. E. B. Du Bois, Martin Luther King, and other male leaders. The museum called Bayard Rustin a master civil rights strategist, but as far as I could tell, it never gave that accolade to any women, even though several deserved that recognition. Yes, the museum talked about Harriet Tubman's legendary achievements as an Underground Railroad conductor, Civil War leader, civil rights activist, and women's suffragist, but I don't think the museum challenged visitors to put Tubman where she belongs—in the same pantheon as "the big boys."

Whenever I have asked people to name great abolitionists and civil rights activists, they have always mentioned Douglass and King. Sometimes, they have also lauded Du Bois and Paul Robeson. They got defensive when I criticized both men for refusing to denounce Stalin and his purge trials. [97] Those who have really done homework on the Civil Rights Movement have lauded Fred Shuttlesworth, the great leader in Birmingham, and have rightly complained that he has

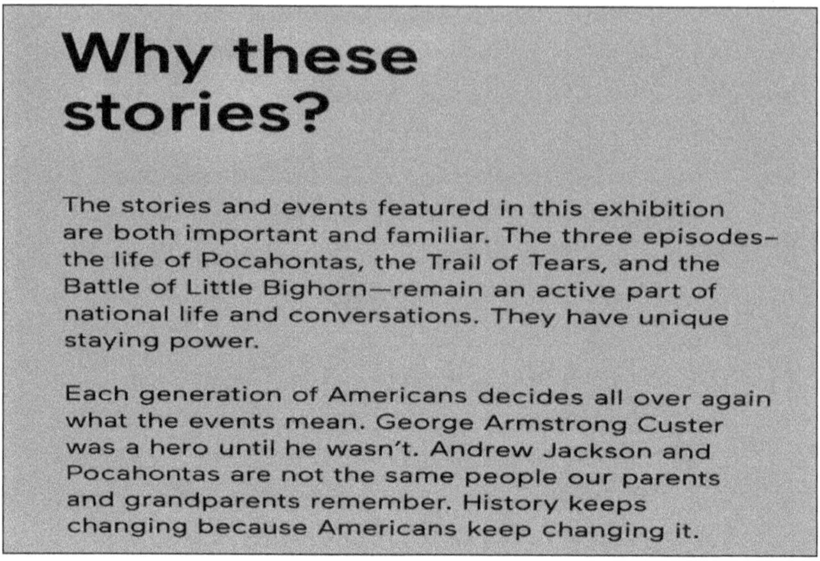

Why these stories?

The stories and events featured in this exhibition are both important and familiar. The three episodes—the life of Pocahontas, the Trail of Tears, and the Battle of Little Bighorn—remain an active part of national life and conversations. They have unique staying power.

Each generation of Americans decides all over again what the events mean. George Armstrong Custer was a hero until he wasn't. Andrew Jackson and Pocahontas are not the same people our parents and grandparents remember. History keeps changing because Americans keep changing it.

Photo by Joanne M. Callahan

Figure 7: Exhibit board at the National Museum of the American Indian.

never gotten all the credit he deserves. When I called these people out on sexism and pressed them to name a woman, they would name—you guessed it—Rosa Parks. But I have NEVER heard anyone put Wells and Tubman in that pantheon. If the museum really wants to honor women, it must "do better," as Michelle Obama would say.

After my experience at the African American museum, I was curious to see how the National Museum of the American Indian treats women. For starters, it has striking architecture, thoughtful exhibits, and outstanding gardens that make me want to spend all day gazing at the greenery overlooking the Capitol dome. The presentation on "The Cult of Pocahontas" and how it continues was insightful and sometimes hilarious. This display brilliantly dissected all the myths we grew up with. The "Why these stories?" exhibit board, seen in Figure 7 above, should be required reading in all American history classes. I love the line, "History keeps changing because Americans keep changing it." If I didn't believe it, I would never take the time to write this book.

However, the National Museum of the American Indian said almost nothing about the Women's Suffrage Movement. The displays paid very little attention to the strong influence that the Haudenosaunee (Iroquois) had on Elizabeth Cady Stanton and other white suffragists. Profiles of Native American suffragists were minimal. They certainly didn't get the attention that Pocahontas got. The museum said that early American society was hierarchal. The presentation should have said patriarchal. I would argue that it is still patriarchal, albeit in a highly modernized way.

The First Americans Museum in Oklahoma City, which I visited in May 2024, didn't just sideline the Women's Suffrage Movement. The museum completely ignored the movement. The museum had an excellent, detailed timeline of American history told from the First Americans' perspective. However, the timeline said nothing about the Seneca Falls Convention in 1848 and the influence of the Haudenosaunee community on white suffragists. Most shockingly, the timeline was silent about ratification of the Nineteenth Amendment in 1920 and the fact that Native American women living on reservations were not able to benefit from the amendment because they were not considered citizens. To ignore those milestones is to say that women's rights don't matter and that women are creampuffs.

Even though there were problems with these museums, I know that there has been progress. When I lived in Birmingham, Alabama, in 2003, I attended a presentation on Ida B. Wells. The lecturer said nothing about her suffrage activism, and nobody called him out on it. When I visited the Harriet Tubman Home and National Historical Park in Auburn, New York, in 2015, I was surprised to find that she was a suffragist who worked with Susan B. Anthony. In my experience, many people thought her women's suffrage activism was such a trivial side issue that they didn't mention it in presentations.

Thanks to decades of intersectional feminist activism, Black, Latina, Asian and Native American suffragists finally started to get the credit they deserve during the Nineteenth Amendment Centennial. I was attracted to the National Votes for Women Trail and the collaborative's marker project partly because of its goal to dedicate 30 percent of markers to suffragists of color. But Mary Church Terrell, Jovita Idar, Mabel Ping-Hua Lee, and other outstanding activists still don't have their own websites, and there is a lot more work to do.

Indeed, when I read about the project to move Rosa Parks's house from Detroit to Berlin, I thought, "When are feminists going to post a historical marker in Berlin that honors the groundbreaking speech that Mary Church Terrell gave in German, French, and English at the International Congress of Women in 1904? Posting a historical marker is a piece of cake compared to moving a house to another country." [98]

We are so used to understating the achievements of suffragists of all races that it feels like we are bragging if we tell the world that we admire them. But this approach often comes across as patronizing, and it's not persuasive enough to get these women into our history textbooks.

Indeed, after we unveiled a National Votes for Women Trail marker for Maud Sampson Williams [99] at the El Paso County Courthouse in 2022, I couldn't stop thinking that something had been missing.

What had been missing was a lack of praise for the great El Pasoan. In her keynote address, civil rights attorney Ouisa D. Davis said that "Maud Sampson Williams didn't just show up for meetings. She was leaven." To call someone leaven is a high compliment, but on its own, the phrase is too understated. Davis should have added something like, "Maud Sampson Williams could walk into a meeting and, by the sheer force of her organizational skills and dynamic personality, she could take the lead and get things done. She was not afraid to push the envelope on crucial issues, even when the time wasn't ripe and there was almost no chance of success. Her groundbreaking women's suffrage, community development, and civil rights activism spanned fifty years and left a tremendous legacy and a compelling mandate for all El Pasoans. We must stop ignoring Williams during Black History Month and Women's History Month and make sure that she gets into the pantheon of great Texans."

I sense that giving suffragists the right amount of praise is something we will need to work on for a long, long time, which begs

Photo by Joanne M. Callahan

Figure 8: Entrance to the Turning Point Suffragist Memorial, with Alice Paul holding a picket sign.

the question, "Did the suffragists in the Occoquan Park memorial and the *Suffs* musical get all the credit they deserved?"

What Was Missing from that Tribute at Occoquan Park?

After a disappointing experience at the Lucy Burns Museum, I wasn't in the mood to visit the Turning Point Suffragist Memorial at Occoquan Park. But the memorial was a five-minute drive from the museum, so I decided to give it a whirl. When I entered the park, the magnificent panorama of hemlock, oak, bald cypress, and Virginia pine trees made me feel like I was entering another world.

As I came closer to the memorial, I got more surprises—a lovely large lake, a Swiss chalet-style visitor center and a nice little café— perfect for a hike or a picnic. And then, I saw an enchanting gem designed by Robert E. Beach Architects, LLC. Alice Paul was holding a picket sign, "Mr. President, how long must women wait for liberty?"

Figure 9: Outside the Turning Point Suffragist Memorial.

As I entered the gates of the memorial, I saw the story of the American Women's Suffrage Movement told in a series of illustrated exhibit boards winding in a circle, from the Seneca Falls Convention in July 1848, the Year of Revolution, all the way up to the present. The exhibit boards also cover the fight for the Voting Rights Act and the ERA from 1923 up to 2020, when Virginia became the thirty-eighth state to ratify it. The boards admit that the ERA has not been certified as part of the Constitution.

The exhibit boards are frank about the Jim Crow culture that suffragists lived in and how it divided activists. But they do not fall into the trap of shaming. NAWSA and NWP had to play realpolitik, and African American suffragists were forced to form their own organizations.

The memorial foregrounds the story of the horrific experiences of incarcerated suffragists at the Occoquan Workhouse not only because the memorial is so close to the prison, but because the suffragists' terrible incarceration was the most definitive turning point in the movement. After the Night of Terror, the days when politicians and the public could trivialize the movement were gone forever.

The memorial notes that Mary Church Terrell, co-founder and

Figure 10: List of suffragists incarcerated at the Occoquan Workhouse.

Photos by Joanne M. Callahan

Figure 11 (left): Mary Church Terrell.
Figure 12 (above): Carrie Chapman
Catt celebrating ratification of the
Nineteenth Amendment with a bouquet.

the first president of the National Association of Colored Women (NACW), picketed the White House with her daughter Phyllis and other NWP members in 1917. However, Terrell was not present on the day when several women were arrested.

The memorial celebrates August 26, 1920, that magical day when the Nineteenth Amendment finally became the law of the land, by placing Carrie Chapman Catt, that virtuoso of practical politics, inside a rotunda, as shown in Figure 12. That seasoned veteran of the Women's

Suffrage Movement, with thirty-three years of experience, is holding a huge, richly deserved bouquet of chrysanthemums and delphiniums.

So after seeing a beautiful memorial with much to offer, what is missing? For starters, it never summarizes the experiences of German American suffragists during World War I. One of the exhibit boards has a picture of imprisoned suffragist Kate Heffelfinger in a severely weakened state. Heffelfinger is a Swiss German name. Did her ancestry have anything to do with the horrendous way she was treated?

After the United States entered WWI, White House protesters were arrested partly because their patriotism was held suspect, like Americans of German lineage. Were suffragists of German descent treated worse than other activists? Even if they weren't treated differently, we need to know. If I had a German surname and had picketed the White House after April 6, 1917, I would be more nervous than if I had a name like Smith or McIntyre.

Alice Paul said there were calls for a congressional investigation because of rumors that the Germans were financing the NWP. However, the NWP was very open about its finances, and Paul joked that "we had so little money that there wasn't much to investigate." [100] That sort of information needs to be included in suffrage exhibits.

But what really offended me were the patronizing statements about suffragists. After seeing so much intellectual brilliance, political savvy, and heroism, the authors of the exhibit boards only commended them for their determination. They would have never treated men as badly.

It was also deeply insulting that the exhibit boards never said that August 26 needs to be a federal holiday; that the Women's Suffrage Movement needs to be taken seriously in every American and world history textbook; and that all major suffrage leaders deserve the Presidential Medal of Freedom.

Because of its location, the memorial only pays homage to suffragists who were imprisoned in the Occoquan Workhouse. However, I hope it inspires a memorial in a high-visibility area of Washington, DC, that pays homage to every imprisoned suffragist. I would want the memorial to be the place for vigils and protests whenever a women's rights activist in, say, Iran or Afghanistan, gets imprisoned. When the Smithsonian American Women's History Museum finally gets built, it needs to have a highly visible outdoor memorial to these heroic suffragists.

Despite the limitations of the Turning Point memorial, I am strongly urging my friends to visit the monument when they're in the DC area. I'm also telling them that no, Turning Point is not in the middle of nowhere.[101]

In the future, women's suffrage memorials need to strongly encourage visitors to become history activists so that these great Americans will finally get the respect they deserve and we don't have to keep educating our progressive friends.

Suffs Gets My Vote,
But Did It Really Honor the Suffragists?

After I saw *Suffs* at the historic Music Box Theatre on Broadway in October 2024, I called skeptical feminist friends throughout the country and told them, "I have nine words to say about the show: *Suffs* gets my vote. Go see it. JUST GO." And then, I elaborated:

> The show was a lot of fun and yes, it was inspiring. I went to the Wednesday matinee and expected to be one of the few in the audience, joined by white boomers and WWII centenarians. But it was a full house with enthusiastic people of all ages and races. Not surprisingly, the musical played fast and loose with a few of the facts, but if we stay away because it's not up to our standards, artists will give up on creating something better because nobody is interested. Hillary Clinton and Malala Yousafzai are not going to produce a show if nobody is going to see it. *Suffs* is like *The Crown*. It whets the appetite.

Suffs has an infectious Broadway musical enthusiasm, and it tells the story of the Women's Suffrage Movement in a way that catches the zeitgeist without trying too hard to be relevant. Songs like "Keep Marching" and lines like "Progress is possible but not guaranteed" are tailor-made for the age of Trump, but they also sound like something Alice Paul would say.

The musical has several clever musical numbers. The "If We Were Married" duet between Dudley Malone and Doris Stevens, with Malone singing along the lines of "I will love you as Christ loved the Church" and Stevens detailing the numerous ways that her economic and legal rights will be severely curtailed, tells a trenchant his-and-hers story of marriage in the early twentieth century. It compels the audience to reflect on how much has changed—and how much has been agonizingly slow to change—in the early twenty-first, especially when they sing the song again towards the end of the show and Carrie Chapman Catt and Mary Garrett Hay join them.

Whether intentional or not, the White House protest scenes made me realize the profound—and profoundly underrated—*chutzpah* it took to be the first activists to stand in that center of American power *without firearms* and silently hold picket signs. In a nation that has always been prone to mass shootings, I was stunned that the suffs weren't carrying pistols, knives, and shotguns.

Suffs inevitably invites comparisons with *Hamilton*, the great innovative musical that took the starch out of Revolutionary War history and made it interesting again. *Hamilton* got well-deserved criticism because the musical glossed over the evils of slavery and Alexander's complicated relationship with "the peculiar institution."

Suffs is more honest about racism in the early twentieth century and how it impacted women's suffrage. But some commentaries on *Suffs* say that the Nineteenth Amendment enfranchised some American women, thus giving the erroneous idea that the amendment was "whites only." Sorry, but the issue is not simple, as I explain in the "White Suffragists, Racism, 'Great Men,' and the Double Standard" section.

Suffs was more moving than *Hamilton*, especially when Alice Paul sang the poignant "Worth It?" and Inez Milholland, Lucy Burns, Ida B. Wells, Mary Church Terrell, and Carrie Chapman Catt joined her in a chorus at the end. I shed a few tears when Inez Milholland died and Alice Paul was put into solitary confinement.

But did *Suffs* really do justice to these great activists? Carrie Chapman Catt comes across much better than in *Iron Jawed Angels*. She is portrayed as a resourceful activist who worked her way through college and devoted her whole life to fighting the good fight. And she will not let brilliant young upstarts cancel her into irrelevancy. But Jenn Colella, the fine actor who played her, showed none of Catt's gravitas.

The same is true of Hawley Gould, who played Alice Paul. Catt was the plucky older woman; Paul was the spunky young lady, completely conforming to the script and to our culture's discomfort with powerful feminist women.

The other activists don't fare better. Inez Milholland was the blatant libertine, even though the real-life Milholland was much more subtle about her open marriage and belief in free love. Mary Church Terrell had none of the "when she walks into a room, she dominates it with her elegance and dignity" quality that I see in her pictures.

Worst of all, Lucy Burns was portrayed as a shy, prim Catholic who would never say, "I'm a great American bitch." Not at all like the real Lucy Burns, the savvy, sociable redhead—so much like a Brooklyn Irish politician, in the best sense of the word.

The audience went wild when, at the end of *Suffs*, a National Organization for Women (NOW) activist interviewed Alice Paul in her older years, and Paul told her to keep marching for ERA.

The NOW activist should have also said, "Alice, you and the other suffs are too modest about your accomplishments. August 26 needs to be a federal holiday, and we all need to get the day off. We need to stand up to history teachers and textbooks that trivialize you. And you, Inez Milholland, Lucy Burns, Ida B. Wells, Mary Church Terrell, and Carrie Chapman Catt—all of you deserve the Presidential Medal of Freedom."

Those lines would have brought the house down. Like *Suffs* itself, I have used the suffragists as inspiration when I'm depressed and need motivation to keep marching in the age of Trump. But it is demeaning to treat great leaders as political therapy tools.

Suffs and all other monuments to these great activists need to insist that our culture treats them with the honor they deserve—without turning them into plaster saints.

In the next chapter, I will give insights into why it is so difficult to perform that basic act of decency.

WHY SUFFRAGISTS GET DENIGRATED

"If you understand the woman suffrage movement in all its complexity, you understand this country."
Paula Giddings, historian [1]

"But how can you embrace what some are trying to cancel?"
Ellen Goodman and Lynn Sherr, journalists [2]

"Mothers and daughters stand divided; how long until we are conquered?"
Rebecca Dakin Quinn, women's studies professor [3]

CHAPTER TWO

When I watched the Paris Olympics closing ceremony and saw Anne Hidalgo, the mayor of Paris, pass the torch to Karen Bass, the mayor of Los Angeles, I smiled and got a dreamy flashback to the last festivities of the Tokyo Olympics, when Yuriko Koike, the governor of Tokyo, handed the reins over to *Madame La Maire*. [4]

After the Olympics ended, I thought about how Elizabeth Cady Stanton and her son Theodore would have been over the moon if they could have seen how much progress we have made in the twentieth and twenty-first centuries. We not only had an equal number of male and female athletes in Paris, something that Theodore could only imagine in his wildest dreams, but three Olympics in the twenty-first century have been led by women mayors around the world.

Nevertheless, suffragists and historical feminists in these countries still struggle to get even half of the respect they deserve. Pundits all over the globe tell ambitious women to keep their feminist activism in the closet, or at least, be understated about it, if they want to get a promotion or to become president of the United States. It's fine for a female candidate to wear a white skirt suit or pantsuit, but she dare not tell the world that Women's Equality Day should be a federal holiday, with a day off.

Obviously, suffragists are getting denigrated because of the double standard and misogyny. Evidence is overwhelming that misogyny can coexist in a world full of empowered women.

But when people attack or patronize suffragists and historical feminists, another dimension comes into play. Many women's history advocates either become passive bystanders or they join in the trashing. In a world where it is *au courant* for even non-feminist women to push back against sexism, why do so many feminists who say they love women's history remain silent when Elizabeth Cady Stanton gets shamed or when people act like Harriet Tubman is inferior to Frederick Douglass?

Against this backdrop, we have a moral imperative to not only expose the double standard but to start showing what a single standard of history looks like.

Two articles in this section point to that fair standard. In the first article, I have used John Blake's "Did Black Lives Matter to Abraham Lincoln? It's Complicated" as a template to show how we can apply the same standard to white suffragists that was applied to Lincoln and famed naturalist John Muir. In the second article, I compared *The Vote* to *The Agitators* in the single-standard sweepstakes and deemed *The Agitators* the winner, albeit an imperfect one. Nevertheless, it's a good play and a lot less inflammatory than Brent Staples's polemics.

The last article in this section discusses Susan Faludi's controversial theory of feminist matricide, whereby contemporary feminists dismiss the accomplishments of their foremothers. The theory is not perfect, but its insights help us understand why suffragists are still getting denigrated in a world of women leaders.

Showing the world a single standard of history and fighting against matricide are powerful tools in the movement to honor suffragists. We need to start using them now.

Racism, White Suffragists, 'Great Men,' and the Double Standard

In July 2020, Michael Brune, former executive director of the Sierra Club, wrote "Pulling Down Our Monuments." In the article, he challenged the organization to reckon with the alleged racism of John Muir and the wealthy white men he associated with, to take down the monuments to him, and to devote itself to environmental justice.

Not surprisingly, the article generated an enormous amount of heat. To its credit, the Sierra Club posted a multitude of responses, both pro and con, on its website.[5] When I, as a Sierra Club Wilderness Guardian, called the concierge for my region and told him that I thought the article was unfair to Muir, I got a good hearing.

The John Muir Global Network wasted no time in defending the environmental pioneer and posted an extensive list of articles making a compelling case that the issue is complicated, and that canceling Muir is unjust.[6] Muir's biographer, Donald Worster, chimed in: "Why did anyone put up a statue of Muir in the first place? Did they mean that here is a human being without moral blemish? There are no such people in the world."[7]

Likewise, whenever someone has accused Abraham Lincoln of racism, the historical cavalry has always come out marching in full force—usually with an academic-sounding plea to stop the presentism, accept Lincoln's complexity, stop treating him like a demigod, and get into the zen of the precarious political and cultural environment

Lincoln lived in. One of my favorite articles on Lincoln and race is John Blake's "Did Black Lives Matter to Abraham Lincoln? It's Complicated." It has a balanced view of the Great Emancipator, and it provides a clear way for a reader to see both the forest and the trees.

However, I was livid when I saw the National Collaborative for Women's History Sites statement on "Women's Suffrage, Historical Markers, and Race":

> As we remember all those who struggled for the right to vote, we also recognize that racism pervaded much of the European American suffrage movement . . .
>
> We recognize that we all share in patterns of systemic racism. Our intent is not to ignore this racism but to open it up for public debate. To leave woman suffragists out of the story because they inherited, benefitted from, and often promoted an entrenched system of white supremacy would be to ignore the complex and pervasive intertwining of gender, race, and class—past and present.[8]

As I read those academic statements, it felt like the authors were flagellating their great-great-grandmothers, and that they wanted us to drown in an ocean of guilt, even though they used the words *entrenched, systemic,* and *inherited.* The collaborative said that it wants to open the issue of suffragists and racism up for public debate. However, I saw no responses to their statement—both pro and con—on its website. I wanted to write a letter, but I feared that I would get ignored, placated, attacked, or canceled.

Unlike John Muir and Abraham Lincoln, white suffragists were hung out to dry. They had no historical cavalry.

Since the collaborative's statement did not have the nuance and depth of John Blake's great article, I decided to draft my own essay. In my piece below, I will use the Blake article as a template but will add to it.

The Suffragists' Legacy Is Complex, Evolving, and Always in Danger of Getting Forgotten

Thanks to the suffragists' hard-won triumph, the largest single expansion of the electorate in the history of this country happened in 1920. However, only 35 percent to 45 percent of American women cast ballots, as opposed to 68 percent of their male counterparts. [9]

Considering the deep restrictions in American society, it's hardly a mystery why so many women could not take advantage of this tremendous achievement: Jim Crow laws; the Ku Klux Klan; Asian immigrants prohibited from becoming citizens; Native Americans who lived on reservations not being counted as citizens; Washington, DC, residents forbidden to vote; men keeping their wives and daughters away from the polls and getting away with it; women who lost their citizenship because they married foreigners; poll taxes; and women who honestly believed that God was against women's suffrage.

And yet, as activists painstakingly lifted most of these obstacles one by one and the culture slowly changed, women's voting rates started to equal those of men and eventually surpass them, and the Nineteenth Amendment laid the groundwork for every feminist/women's rights achievement in the twentieth and twenty-first centuries. Both Democrats and Republicans actively court women's votes. Democratic presidential candidates Hillary Clinton and Kamala Harris lost the Electoral College, but Clinton won the popular vote by over two million in 2016 and Harris lost by only 1.6 percent in 2024, providing evidence that arguably, this country is almost ready for a woman president. [10]

Nevertheless, the Women's Suffrage Movement has always been in danger of getting thrown into the ash heap of history. As we all know, Women's Equality Day is still not a federal holiday and history textbooks pay scant attention to suffragists. Some people seem to enjoy lambasting them.

Ten years ago, whenever I talked about suffragists, someone would always scapegoat them for Prohibition and insist that I talk about their views on temperance. There has always been a bias that the complex temperance movement was all about "sexually frustrated church ladies" who had a fixation against beer and wine. This bias was so widespread that political science professor Mark Lawrence Schrad wrote "Why Do We Blame Women for Prohibition?" [11]

But one article would never be enough to stop the carping. Historians and battered women's advocates had to keep telling contemporary Americans, "It's complicated."

They had to keep reminding us about married women's reality in the nineteenth and early twentieth centuries. They had to highlight activists like Ohio suffrage leader Harriet Taylor Upton, who proclaimed, "There will be no union of forces with the drys this fall to secure our equal rights amendment to the constitution." [12]

Above all, they had to tell the world that women played a huge role in *ending* Prohibition. The Women's Organization for National Prohibition Reform, led by the politically savvy New York socialite Pauline Sabin, was one of the most powerful forces against the failed "noble experiment." [13]

But just as soon as the pillorying about Prohibition stopped and women's history advocates were dealing with COVID lockdowns and the Nineteenth Amendment Centennial, George Floyd was murdered, and Black Lives Matter rightly challenged all Americans to examine our country's racist legacy. They immediately intensified the strobe light on white suffragists, including the multitudes who were abolitionists.

As I read all the accusations and heard about the campaigns to cancel Carrie Chapman Catt and Alice Paul at, respectively, Iowa State University and the University of Pennsylvania, I thought, "Here we go again. People will never stop trying to dump suffragists into the dustbin."

It took a long time for historians and battered women's advocates to set the record straight on the complexities of suffrage and Prohibition, and we need to do the same thing on racism.

Why Many Say White Suffragists Were Racists

Those who argue that white suffragists were racist point to statements and actions of the leaders, especially Elizabeth Cady Stanton, Susan B. Anthony, Alice Paul, and Carrie Chapman Catt. They also emphasize the segregation in suffrage organizations.

The mainstream and progressive media are loaded with posts about the cringeworthy statements of white suffragists. They have a huge impact on how people perceive these activists. When I started talking to a seventeen-year-old self-identified feminist about Elizabeth Cady Stanton, she interrupted, "She was a racist." And then she quoted Stanton's statement, "Think of Patrick and Sambo and Hans and Yung Tung who do not know the difference between a monarchy and a republic, who never read the Declaration of Independence or Webster's spelling book, making laws for Lydia Marie Child, Lucretia Mott, or Fanny Kimble."

I have heard people accuse Susan B. Anthony of being a dilettante abolitionist because of her shocking tirade: "I will cut off this right arm of mine before I will ever work for or demand the ballot for the Negro and not the woman." It didn't matter to them that she took tremendous risks and had to face violent hecklers during her anti-slavery campaigns.

Carrie Chapman Catt's infamous "White supremacy will be strengthened, not weakened, by women's suffrage" continues to be used as proof that she was an unrepentant racist.

It is almost guaranteed that someone will mention racism nowadays at a suffragist event. Every time I have listened to a speech about Alice Paul's leadership of the 1913 parade, the part that has received the most emphasis was the fact that she told Black suffragists to march at the back.

Almost every suffrage commemoration I have attended since 2020 has pointed out the segregation in the movement. During the unveiling of a National Votes for Women Trail marker in October 2022 at Wooldridge Square Park in Austin, Texas, former Austin Parks and Recreation leader Gloria Mata Pennington gave a short speech about segregation in the movement. City Council Member Kathie Tovo told the audience to stop ignoring Black suffragists. If she or her staff had done some research, she would have found out that we had unveiled a Maud Sampson Williams marker in El Paso in March and that the National Votes for Women Trail is committed to a goal of awarding 30 percent of markers to suffragists of color.

The comments at the Austin unveiling brought back flashbacks to memorials I had attended for WWII veterans and civil rights leaders. I have NEVER heard one word about segregation in the WWII military at any event honoring heroes of the Greatest Generation, even when the event had veterans of all races. I certainly never got a lecture on Martin Luther King's marital infidelities and sexism at the civil rights events I have attended. Of all the places in Texas for the double standard of history to rear its ugly head, it just had to happen on "the blueberry in the tomato soup," as Governor Rick Perry referred to Austin.

Why Many Say White Suffragists Were Not Racists

Those who argue that white suffragists were not racists emphasize historical context, the severe difficulty of getting most women's voting rights laws on the books, and the double standard.

They remind us that the suffragists' early dream was for women and Blacks to attain their voting rights together, even though most Americans were rabidly against it. They reiterate that Anthony and Stanton started the groundbreaking Women's Loyal National League, which was instrumental in passing the Thirteenth Amendment—the law that made slavery illegal in this country—but that they were jolted into playing realpolitik after the Civil War.

"How could they have gone from devoted abolitionism to racism?" wondered Ta-Nehisi Coates, as quoted by Myriam Miedzian. "I find myself in sympathy for both Stanton and Anthony, who after devoting so much of their early lives to abolitionism, hoped for some reciprocity which did not come . . . I don't need my personal pantheon to be clean. But I need it to be filled with warriors." [14]

In contrast, historians tell us to take the abolitionists' sexism in cultural context and excuse Frederick Douglass's patronizing comments to Anthony and Stanton about women's suffrage, including his shocking statement that slave women are oppressed not because they are women but because they are Black.

They also give Douglass a pass on his racist and xenophobic comments about, respectively, Native Americans and Irish immigrants, and his support of a former Confederate general instead of a progressive Black jurist in the 1888 congressional election. David Blight, author of the Pulitzer Prize-winning biography of the legendary abolitionist, calls Douglass "beautifully human" when discussing his flaws. [15]

However, Alice Paul and Carrie Chapman Catt don't get any passes, and they're hardly considered "beautifully human." We rarely hear about the wrenching dilemma that Alice Paul faced when the public found out that Howard University students would march in the 1913 suffrage parade. In her own words:

> I began to receive letters from many, many, many, many splendid supporters we had, saying, "This is unheard of. We are certainly not going to come up and march in a procession where you have colored women marching."
>
> It reached the newspapers, and they played it up to the utmost, to get dissension sowed in our ranks. It was quite a problem. It was extremely difficult because we had so many women saying, "There will be nobody from our town, there will be nobody from our state to do this," then lots coming forth in the newspapers inflaming everybody about the subject. It was a very difficult situation. [16]

Since the American Women's Suffrage Movement was still recovering from the doldrums, including the backlash after the Titanic disaster, and it needed all the support it could get for a constitutional amendment, it is understandable—and profoundly painful—why Paul compromised and told Black women to march at the back. Activists have always engaged in realpolitik, but suffragists get judged more harshly for it.

In the proof-text poker game regarding Carrie Chapman Catt's "true" views on race, one fact almost always gets trivialized. She stood up to *der Führer*. Shortly after Hitler rose to power, Catt organized the Protest Committee of Non-Jewish Women Against the Persecution of Jews in Germany. In 1933, the group sent a protest letter signed by nine thousand American women to the League of Nations and to newspapers in countries bordering Germany.[17] Because of this stunning act of resistance, Catt was the first woman to get the American Hebrew Medal. If the Nazis had ever occupied this country, Catt would have been arrested.[18]

Likewise, pundits rarely mention that Alice Paul, when she lived in Switzerland, helped Jewish refugees get American visas and escape to the United States as quickly as possible.[19]

Against this backdrop, it is hardly surprising that the media generally ignores these crucial facts:

> • The Southern States Woman Suffrage Conference was originally part of NAWSA but broke off in 1904 because it explicitly believed in whites-only suffrage and states' rights.[20]

> • W. E. B. Du Bois and Mary Church Terrell wrote that Carrie Chapman Catt was "without racial prejudice."[21] Ida B. Wells was a guest at Susan B. Anthony's house.[22] Frederick Douglass was a frequent dinner guest at Elizabeth Cady Stanton's and Susan B. Anthony's homes.[23]

> • Elizabeth Cady Stanton openly supported Frederick Douglass's highly controversial interracial marriage to Helen Pitts and sent them a letter of congratulations.[24]

• Carrie Chapman Catt opposed efforts to insert the word "white" into the Nineteenth Amendment. She also supported the Committee on One Hundred, a prominent organization in New York City that called upon Congress to enforce the Fifteenth Amendment, which enfranchised African American men. [25]

• Several Black suffragists were members of NAWSA, NWP, the National Woman's Suffrage Association (NWSA) and the American Women's Suffrage Association (AWSA). Sharon Harley notes that "Hattie Purvis was a delegate to the NWSA (as well as a member of the executive committee of the Pennsylvania State Suffrage Association). Among the prominent African American reformers and suffragists who joined the AWSA were Charlotte Forten and Josephine St. Pierre Ruffin, a member of the Massachusetts Woman Suffrage Association." [26]

When I first heard that the Women's Suffrage Movement was segregated, I thought it meant that Black women could only join African American suffrage organizations, that they were always forbidden to join white-dominated groups in every region of the country. I was surprised to find out about the activists mentioned above. When historians and journalists talk about segregation in the movement, they need to clearly describe their terms.

All these facts provide strong evidence that suffragists are the victims of a movement that sees racism in progressive white historical figures as an either/or proposition—either you're a racist or you're not. [27] This rigidity not only weaponizes history; more importantly, it keeps the world from seeing how the suffrage movement benefitted all American women.

What Did the Nineteenth Amendment
Do for the Civil Rights Movement?

When I found out that Mississippi didn't ratify the Nineteenth Amendment until 1984 and that North Carolina, Florida, Georgia, Louisiana, and South Carolina didn't ratify it until 1969-1971, I wondered what would have happened if the Nineteenth Amendment had never made it into the Constitution and individual states had stopped passing suffrage laws after 1920. We would have still had women of all races voting in states like New York, Illinois, and California, but they would have been disenfranchised in many Southern states and in states like Delaware.

Without the Nineteenth Amendment, the Civil Rights Act of 1965 would have been only for men in states that did not allow women to vote. Why? Because the Supreme Court did not start applying the equal protection clause of the Fourteenth Amendment to sex discrimination issues until 1971, in the landmark *Reed v. Reed* case.[28] Many people hate to admit it, but the Nineteenth Amendment did something for the Civil Rights Movement.

After 1920, there was no question that women would be included in all future voting rights laws. If American women had been forced to keep fighting for the amendment until 1944 or 1971 (the years when French and Swiss women, respectively, won the vote), the Civil Rights Movement would have had to keep dealing with the woman issue.[29]

Pundits rightly tell us that initially white women, especially affluent Anglo-Saxon Protestants, benefitted the most from the Nineteenth Amendment. But they also need to admit that many other women voted in 1920: Maclovia Uresti, one of the first women to vote in Victoria, Texas;[30] several Black women outside the South, including Ida B. Wells;[31] my working-class Irish and Italian Catholic immigrant grandmothers; and a few Black women in Tennessee before Jim Crow hardliners cracked down and prevailed. Indeed, the voter registration card of Isabella Ewing, a Black resident of Nashville, was displayed in the July 2020 NYT article, "My ____ was a Suffragist."[32] An untitled article in the *Clarksville Leaf-Chronicle* notes that two "colored" women voted in the 1920 election.[33]

There is a misconception that African Americans never voted until the passage of the Voting Rights Act of 1965 and that the Fifteenth and Nineteenth Amendments were meaningless to them. However, in several states outside the South, Black women and men did vote and many cast ballots for Republicans.[34] A few Black men were politicians. Arthur Mitchell and Adam Clayton Powell Jr. were Democratic congressmen from, respectively, Illinois's First Congressional District (mainly the south side of Chicago) and Harlem. Mitchell was in Congress from 1935 to 1943, Powell from 1945 to 1971. Ida B. Wells ran for the Illinois state senate in 1930 and lost.[35]

Archibald Carey gave a speech at the 1952 Republican Convention and his words echo in Martin Luther King's "I Have a Dream."[36]

When stating that African American women and men could vote in states that didn't adhere to Jim Crow laws, I am not trying to trivialize the Voting Rights Act. That landmark legislation was absolutely necessary to make every state in the union enforce the Fifteenth and Nineteenth Amendments.

Unfortunately, most articles on the Voting Rights Act ignore the women's suffrage amendment and say something like "[it] offered African Americans a way to circumvent state and local barriers that prevented them from exercising their *Fifteenth Amendment* right to vote."[37]

Even during the Roaring Twenties, the heyday of the Ku Klux Klan, there were glimmers of what the Nineteenth Amendment could do for women of color and female immigrants. It's a shame that people ignore them. This bruising, no-win fight about racism and white suffragists is not only straining the women's history movement, it tells me that we're asking the wrong questions about these great activists. To quote Lincoln historian Eric Foner, "If you ask the wrong question, you're going to get the wrong answer."[38]

The Questions We Need to Ask

Towards the end of "Did Black Lives Matter to Abraham Lincoln? It's Complicated," John Blake implied that proof-text poker games about Lincoln's racism are not going to solve America's polarization problem. He then reflected on what made Lincoln a great president. In that spirit, I am going to answer the same question about suffragists in the "Fighting Back" chapter. Blake urged us to embrace Lincoln's "splendid inconsistencies" and "contradictions and ambiguities," especially in our current all-or-nothing political culture. [39]

I end this essay with three questions. Most of us have no problem calling John Muir and Abraham Lincoln great, heroic Americans while acknowledging their "splendid inconsistencies." We can admit that they absorbed the racism of their culture like secondhand smoke—just like everyone else. We can accept the fact that sometimes they made shocking racist remarks, and at other times, they were forced to play realpolitik. And we can affirm those moments when they stood up to racism.

When are we going to affirm the same complexity, the same "splendid inconsistencies" and "contradictions and ambiguities" in Elizabeth Cady Stanton, Susan B. Anthony, Alice Paul, Carrie Chapman Catt, and other white suffragists? Do we need to go on a journey and do another hundred years of activism for that transcendental moment to happen? What is it going to take for our culture to start affirming the same humanity in great historic women that they so eagerly affirm in the world's "great men"?

The Vote v. *The Agitators*:
Who Has the Single Standard?

In 2020, PBS released a superb two-part Michelle Ferrari documentary, *The Vote*. With riveting historical footage and powerful cinematic sweep, it told the story of the American Women's Suffrage Movement, from the Seneca Falls Convention to the ratification of the Nineteenth Amendment, through the eyes of Harriot Stanton Blatch,

Alice Paul, Carrie Chapman Catt, and Ida B. Wells, always treating them as deeply human rock-star activists.

The Vote skillfully combined the tension of a thriller with the introspection of a documentary. Even though I knew how the tale would end, I still felt nervous for the suffragists because the cast and crew were such great storytellers. *The Vote* respected the complexities of the temperance issue and showed how much Alice Paul and Carrie Chapman Catt needed each other, even though they were hardly the best of friends. It didn't shy away from messy conflicts that plague all social movements, including racism.

So after all this rhapsodizing about *The Vote*, why won't I recommend it as a step to a single standard? Why am I recommending a little-known play about the long, respectful, but stormy friendship between Susan B. Anthony and Frederick Douglass?

Because *The Vote*, even with all its strengths, doesn't really challenge the double standard of history. Mary Walton, the esteemed journalist, enthusiastically admits that Alice Paul was a public relations genius, [40] and several academics acknowledge the suffragists' brilliance and heroism. But they NEVER say that Women's Equality Day should be a federal holiday. Those academics are completely silent about our history textbooks' threadbare treatment of the suffrage movement, even though several admitted that they hate it when people say, "Women were granted the vote."

What really irritated me about *The Vote* was that it let Frederick Douglass off the hook. It eagerly repeated Susan B. Anthony's and Elizabeth Cady Stanton's racist remarks when they found out that abolitionists after the Civil War were going to put Black men's voting rights first. But they never told us Frederick Douglass's sexist remarks. [41]

We never heard that Douglass thought women didn't need the vote as much as Black men because their husbands could "protect them and advocate for them," and that slave women were oppressed not because they were women, but because they were Black. We certainly never heard Sojourner Truth's retort:

> There is a great stir about colored men getting their rights, but not a word about the colored women, and if colored men get their rights, and not colored women theirs, you see the colored men will be masters over the women, and it will be just as bad as it was before. [42]

The Vote is too good to cancel, but I'm not going to ignore its deliberate blind spots either.

I first heard about *The Agitators* in 2018, when I complained about the Brent Staples article to other women's history advocates. A Susan B. Anthony fan told me about the play and said it was "very interesting." However, when someone calls something interesting, I usually lose interest. It's usually a cover for "I don't know what to think of it."

So I forgot about *The Agitators* until I started doing research for this book. I found out that Mat Smart was inspired to write the play when he saw a statue of Susan and Frederick having tea at Susan B. Anthony Square in Rochester. Since no theatre company in the Dallas area had performed *The Agitators*, I looked for performances on the internet, but the only one I found was a six-episode podcast. [43]

The podcast was enjoyable, it had good music, and I cried during the last episode. I disagreed with Peter Marks's *Washington Post* review of a local performance, where he said the play felt like an "awfully bland and protracted affair." [44] I was relieved that several commenters pushed back:

> I'm not sure I saw the same production as the critic. I was engaged and inspired . . . Every high school history student should see this play.
>
> —KevMett [45]

> I can't help wondering if the reviewer is lacking the imagination it takes for someone unaffected to feel the anguish of women and Blacks.
>
> —Bobbie Gottschalk [46]

The Agitators doesn't have the élan of *The Vote*. However, it doesn't give Frederick Douglass a pass on his sexist remarks and his patriarchal marriage—even by nineteenth century standards—to Anna Murray Douglass. It also helps us see why both activists had to play realpolitik. In a patriarchal, racist country that rejected an "everyone gets liberated together" approach to social justice in the nineteenth and early twentieth centuries, it is easy to understand why abolitionists pushed for Black male suffrage first after the Civil War; why NAWSA looked the other way when Southern chapters were blatantly segregated; and why Anthony did not want Douglass to speak at a suffrage convention in Atlanta.

The Agitators gives insights on why it was almost impossible for Anthony and Douglass to be philosophical about these political facts of life. They sensed that, at some level, activists were using realpolitik as a smokescreen.

Even though Douglass supported women's suffrage, how could Anthony ever believe that he was always going to be a reliable ally when Anna Murray Douglass made all the sacrifices in the marriage, and when he didn't apologize for his sexist remarks? These facts, along with his alleged infidelities, tell me that Douglass is overrated as a women's rights man. Likewise, Anthony took tremendous physical risks as an abolitionist but was clueless when Douglass told her about the dangers that Black men and their families face, even in progressive Rochester in the 1870s.

The Agitators was a good play, but it would have been much more incisive if it had delved more into Anthony's activism, understood "mothers' realities" in the nineteenth century, and had acknowledged the elephant in the room. I was appalled when *The Agitators*—just like *The Vote*, the Lucy Burns Museum, the Turning Point Suffragist Memorial, Ken Burns's *The Civil War*, and Steven Spielberg's *Lincoln*—ignored Susan B. Anthony and Elizabeth Cady Stanton's leadership of the Women's Loyal National League during the Civil War.

They led the largest petition drive in the nation's history up to that time and Anthony was the chief organizer. Two thousand petition collectors[47] gathered four hundred thousand signatures.[48] Sen. Charles Sumner credited the league as the driving force behind the Thirteenth Amendment.[49] The league punched holes in the nineteenth century stereotype that women were not interested in politics, and it became a template for women's political organizations after the Civil War.

It is historical malpractice for so many historical groups to ignore such a monumental achievement. No wonder Stanton and Anthony were so angry when "pro-woman" abolitionists took a Black men-first stance and told suffragists to wait their turn.

When Susan B. Anthony told Frederick Douglass in *The Agitators* that Anna Murray Douglass never learned to read and write because he never helped her with housework and childcare, I rolled my eyes. Men who just help are still guilty of domestic exploitation. I certainly didn't expect Anthony to use twenty-first century phrases like emotional labor, equal responsibility, and "the mental load," but it would have been appropriate for her to say, "Take initiative in caring for the home. Your family will still have enough to eat if you don't travel all the time, and you'll still be a legend." And it certainly would have been in character for her to display her sadness about the numerous women who "retired" from suffrage activism when they got married.

When I mentioned "the elephant"—you guessed it, I was thinking of the unthinkable: Douglass's rumored infidelities and Anthony's alleged lesbianism. Until recently, biographers thought these rumors were prevalent because of internecine smear campaigns and nineteenth century stereotypes about Black men and suffragists.

Thanks to Maria Diedrich's book *Love Across Color Lines* and other authors' articles about Douglass's affairs and Anthony flirting with other women and calling abolitionist Anna Dickinson her "Chicky Dicky Darling," biographers nowadays can't ignore these allegations. Even David Blight admits that Douglass may have had a twenty-seven-year affair with Ottilie Assing, a radical, left-wing German immigrant who committed suicide after he married Helen Pitts.[50] Regardless of how playwrights treat Douglass's private life, historians will always passionately defend him, even when acknowledging his flaws. David Blight idolizes Douglass even when he's criticizing him. But for Anthony and her rumored lesbianism, the stakes are higher.

The Vote should have acknowledged the queer women in the suffrage movement,[51] and *The Agitators* needs to stop ignoring the elephant. However, I don't want the discussion to make suffragists even more vulnerable to getting dumped into the dustbin. In an age when *Rustin* can be open about the great civil rights activist's homosexuality, I still fear that the issue could get weaponized. Perhaps a playwright could take *The Crown* approach, where we got hints about Prince Philip's infidelities and Queen Elizabeth's affair with Porchy, but it let audience members draw their own conclusions, and it didn't dominate the series.

I would like *The Agitators* to go on a nationwide tour if and only if it contains all my suggested changes. One thing that bothers me about all the positive reviews of *The Agitators* is that nobody called out the double standard of history in so many other accounts of Anthony and Douglass's friendship, including David Blight's book. Mat Smart needs to talk to the media about that misogyny and how he tried to overcome it.

In an age when Hillary Clinton and Michelle and Barack Obama are producing movies and documentaries, they should hire Michelle Ferrari and Mat Smart and turn *The Agitators* into either a multi-part documentary or a TV series. During the pandemic, I discovered several great movies and TV series about German history, from the Kaiser Wilhelm era to Reunification. German filmmakers admit that their history has tremendous built-in drama, and audiences around the world eat it up. And, yes, it provides a multitude of cautionary tales.

Likewise, audiences around the globe are fascinated with the Civil War and its aftermath. We need to take advantage of it, in a good way, and *The Agitators* could provide a great way to set this country on the path to a single standard of history.

Suffragists and Faludi's
Theory of Matricide

It was a conversation I have had way too often. In July 2022, a female IT director told me that even though she is a Democrat, she identifies with Nikki Haley because Haley "deals with the same sexist BS as I do and we're always fighting it alone. But it's always inspiring and fun to see her pushing back against the boys."

I laughed and told her I understood. Then I asked her how she was going to commemorate the upcoming anniversary of the Seneca Falls conference. Her response, after a long, long pause: "I appreciate what those women did for me, but they just don't inspire me and they feel like my great-great-grandmothers. Why should I do anything for them?"

I then told her that when someone attacks or ignores Elizabeth Cady Stanton and other historical feminists, I get angry because it feels like they are attacking *my* mother, and that I do something for these great women to pay my respects. A few weeks after that deflating conversation, I got a "click" when listening to an interview with NYT columnist Michelle Goldberg on the *Ezra Klein Show*:

> I also think there's something specific to feminism that's matricidal, right, where sort of every generation reacts against the generation before it . . . And there's contempt for aging in our society, but there's a very special contempt for aging women. [52]

That conversation not only helped me understand my frustrating chat with the Nikki Haley fan, but it also brought back memories of "American Electra: Feminism's Ritual Matricide," Susan Faludi's highly controversial essay, posted six years before Trump first ran for president. Faludi gave examples of conflicts between older and younger activists that felt like earthquakes on the San Andreas Fault. Then she asked, "Why does so much of 'new' feminist activism and scholarship spurn the work and ideas of the generation that came before?"[53] She proclaimed:

> Women's studies was originally envisioned as the
> repository of feminist history and memory, where
> accumulated knowledge would be enshrined in a safe
> box where future generations could go to retrieve
> it. That academic mother lode is in danger of being
> decommissioned . . .[54]

Faludi does mention the Women's Suffrage Movement, which in her estimation had a respectful mother-daughter dynamic because in early, rural America, "the model republican woman was a mother."[55] She says that the relationship was strained as this country became more industrialized and "scientific child-rearing experts" (almost always men) continuously lashed out at mothers.

The changes were all too obvious in the way some feminists referred to Mama. Frances Willard was addressed as "Mother," and Elizabeth Cady Stanton's most popular speech was "Our Girls." But not too long after, flappers were rolling their eyes at their suffragist moms; Betty Friedan was saying she didn't want to be like her mother; and Jennifer Baumgardner and Amy Richards were proclaiming in the year 2000, "Thou Shalt Not Become Thy Mother."[56]

Feminists did not take Faludi's article sitting down. Men's rights activists and other anti-feminists could hardly hide their glee.

Many responses were so defensive that they came close to trashing, but several made good points: All social movements have generation gaps; it's time to stop dividing feminist activism into waves; the mother-daughter model is patriarchal.

And several activists attempted to bridge the San Andreas Fault. Judith Warner, Emily Baxter, and Milia Fisher reminded us, "The women of Generation X and Millennial women inherited a very different world than those of the Silent Generation and the Baby Boomers."[57] What in the world would they say about Generation Z?

It's risky to say it and I don't want to incite an earthquake, but considering how badly suffragists have been treated, we should revisit Faludi's theory.

The misogyny directed at suffragists and other historical feminists reminds me so much of mother hatred that I can't resist calling it matricide.

I know several people will push back with "I'm sick of parsing feminism along mother-daughter lines." They have a point.

But like it or not, people around the world apply parental metaphors to their nation and to the founders of social movements so often that it seems like a hard-wired instinct: *ma patrie*; *mein vaterland*; George Washington, father of this nation; John Muir, father of the conservation movement; Hermine Tobolowsky, mother of the Texas ERA; Dorothy Height, godmother of the Civil Rights Movement; Rachael Glashan Rupisan saying, "The progress our mothers and grandmothers fought so hard to achieve." [58]

To top it off, the world has a cruel double standard of parenting. Feminists have done a tremendous job of analyzing and documenting the domestic exploitation of mothers and showing how deeply our culture perpetuates the mommy tax and the daddy bonus, that great phrase coined by Ann Crittenden. As Maria Mies said so brilliantly: "Women's labor is considered a natural resource, freely available like air and water." [59]

Gloria Steinem herself wondered about the tendency to treat feminism "as a gigantic mother who is held responsible for almost everything, while the patriarchy receives terminal gratitude for the small favors it bestows." [60]

Indeed, Steinem's quote brought back memories of when I was in the corporate world and I saw women in executive positions profusely thank their male bosses and husbands for being supportive but NEVER give any credit to suffragists and feminists, both deceased and living, even though they sacrificed a thousand times more for these women.

It also brought back memories of numerous women's history sites that comply with the double standard. The National Women's History Alliance (NWHA) says it is "dedicated to promoting and preserving the history of women's contributions to society,"[61] a statement that gives me the impression that women's contributions are not half as good as those of men but that they still deserve honorable mention.

NWHA should have said, "Dedicated to preserving and promoting the history of *women's outstanding, often underrated and forgotten* contributions to society."

Many would call the put-downs of suffragists just another example of canceling, trashing, and misogyny. I am quite open to the view that fundamentally, this "matricide" is women's misplaced anger at men. But we live in a world that tells men who just help out with housework and childcare and "give Mom a break" that they're fabulous fathers. We also live in a world where, of all places, most women's history sites are too timid to REALLY toot the horn of great suffragists and historic feminists. Terms like trashing and misogyny sound too general. The denigration of suffragists feels like matricide to me, and a feminist therapist would have a good time analyzing it.

Regardless of what you or I call the historical double standard, we can't ignore the fact that if women keep seeing their suffragist and feminist foremothers getting trashed or patronized while feminists and women's history advocates remain silent, they're not going to join the movement. No woman wants her work to be treated like a freely available natural resource.

Would Alice Paul and the Silent Sentinels have gone to prison if they knew so many beneficiaries were going to put them down during the Nineteenth Amendment Centennial? Would Carrie Chapman Catt and other suffragists have worked as hard if they had known how badly they were going to be treated in the year 2020? I suspect they still would have done it, but they would have done a lot more to minimize the risk of historical malpractice.[62]

Armed with Faludi's theory of feminist matricide, if I were to have the conversation about Seneca Falls with the Nikki Haley fan today, I would push back a lot harder than I did a few years ago. I would ask, "You seem to be against suffragists because they remind you of your great-great-grandmother. Well, what was so bad about her? Would you knock down nineteenth century labor activists if they reminded you of your imperfect great-great-grandfather? Was your great-great-grandmother a suffragist? If yes, I strongly urge you to honor her activism."

I would also ask, "Why don't the women and men of Seneca Falls inspire you?" I would let her explain and she would probably say that she read boring articles and saw amateurish skits. I would probably respond, "I so badly wish that Greta Gerwig and the cast and crew of *Little Women* and *Barbie* would make a great movie about Seneca Falls. But I have read stories and seen clunky skits about Seneca Falls that have none of the magic of Gerwig's *Little Women*, and yet, I still felt inspired."

I would also urge that woman, and others, to think of the intellectual brilliance and sheer *chutzpah* it took to say in a Wesleyan church on a hot July day in 1848, "We hold these truths to be self-evident, that all men *and women* are created equal," and to write a poignant and concise Declaration of Sentiments that is still relevant today.

Elizabeth Cady Stanton had no organizing and public speaking experience, and yet, she led one of the most revolutionary events of 1848, a year of numerous pro-democracy revolts throughout Europe. She had a long, brilliant career as a theorist, public speaker, writer, and organizer. She even ran for Congress in 1866, and don't forget that she had seven children. Yes, it was fun to watch Nikki Haley when she first ran for president, but when I want real inspiration, I look to Lizzy and the suffs. If people don't like her because she reminds them of their great-great-grandmothers, whom they never met, they need to get their heads examined.

STOP THE MATRICIDE.

FIGHTING BACK

"Suffrage isn't 'boring history.' It is the story of political geniuses. And by the way, it's suffragist, not suffragette."
Jessica Bennett and Veronica Chambers, journalists [1]

"When we change our stories, we change the world."
Anita Sarkeesian and Laura Hudson, feminist bloggers [2]

"Women's anger spurs creativity and drives innovation in politics and social change, and it always has."
Rebecca Traister, author, Good and Mad:
The Revolutionary Power of Women's Anger [3]

Chapter Three

During a dinner conversation with friends in 2023, we started discussing the America250 project. We immediately noticed that on the official website, there was a clip of Martin Luther King but nothing about the women's suffrage and feminist movements. [4]

We all wondered when the women's history movement will fight back. During the Nineteenth Amendment Centennial, suffragists got a lot of mud thrown at them, but most women's history advocates remained silent.

Are they going to act that way during America250?

We conceded that when dealing with museums, historical commissions, universities, and government bureaucracies, you need to be diplomatic. But we all know that when "great men" get attacked, historians have no problem showing their anger and pushing back.

I talked about this issue with a friend who has been involved in all types of historic restoration. She admitted that because of the way most women have been socialized, we often have a frustrating poverty mentality: Be grateful for anything you get, even if it treats suffragists like they're second-rate; anything is better than nothing; suffragists really don't deserve to be admired.

During the dinner party, we asked ourselves, "Have women's history advocates *ever* fought back? And have they fought back in an outspoken way instead of the ladylike 'It's just a suggestion' sort of way?"

I'm here to tell you that yes, they have. This section will give three examples: when advocates built a series of suffrage memorials in Tennessee; when advocates pushed back hard as conservatives tried to convince the world that Susan B. Anthony was an anti-abortion activist; and when the cancel-culture crowd failed to rename Catt Hall at Iowa State University.

But first, we need to answer the question, "What made the suffragists not just remarkable but great?" In a world that views the suffs as remarkable but flawed women who were inferior to "great men," telling the world why they were great is an essential aspect of fighting back.

Answering the Long-Overdue Question: What Made the Suffragists Great?

Suffragists have been unfairly canceled for Prohibition, for racism, for not looking like movie stars, you name it. And yet, because their achievement was so momentous, the public has never been able to completely dump them into the dustbin.

Pundits will patronize the suffragists and say that they were persistent, brave, and creative. However, they could have never achieved the near-impossible over a seventy-year timeframe on persistence alone. The Silent Sentinels who repeatedly went to prison and got tortured were not just brave. When men do that sort of thing, it's called heroism. It's long overdue to ask, "What made those women great?"

But before we get into specifics, we need this reality check:

> Today it is difficult to understand how completely radical the idea of any rights for women was to people of the past. While most people believe they would have supported woman suffrage, the reality is that most of us would not have done so, especially in the early years when that support would have made us social pariahs. [5]

With that humble admission in mind, let's tell the world what made the suffs not just remarkable but as great as the "great men."

They Were Intellectually Brilliant

When I was at Seneca Falls and read the Declaration of Rights and Sentiments, I was stunned by its concise descriptions of so many issues that impact all women and by how relevant it remains today, showing again that to be a suffragist in 1848, you had to be an intellectual and social visionary.

Soraya Chemaly, the director of the Women's Media Center Speech Project, quipped that most people wouldn't recognize the declaration "if it fell on them and squashed them flat." [6] She argues that many of the items identified as women's rights problems in the Declaration of Sentiments are still problems today. [7]

It's staggering to realize how much they hold up a mirror to contemporary America:

- **"He has never permitted her to exercise her inalienable right to the elective franchise."** As a white, middle-class single woman, it is easy for me to go out and vote. But if I were a Black, Hispanic, or Asian American working-class woman, or if I was a Native American woman living on a reservation, it would be quite another story. If extreme right-wingers get their way, it may also be "quite another story" for married women in the future.

- **"He has made her, if married, in the eye of the law, civilly dead."** Twenty-first century married women are not civilly dead, but we have so many vestiges of that mentality that this statement is still relevant. I have even heard female pastors say at the end of wedding ceremonies, "Introducing Mr. and Mrs. His First Name, His Last Name." So we think we have made such tremendous progress since 1848, eh?

- **"In the covenant of marriage, she is compelled to promise obedience to her husband."** In conservative houses of worship nowadays, brides seldom say "obey" at weddings. But as Zawn Villines, owner of the Liberating Motherhood site, said so well: "Sexism is the core problem in most heterosexual relationships." [8] Those highly publicized gaps in housework, childcare, emotional labor, sexual satisfaction, and career advancement benefit husbands at their wives' expense.

- **"He closes against her all the avenues to wealth and distinction, which he considers most honorable to himself."** This one makes me think of Elon Musk and the "boy kings" of Silicon Valley. True, a handful of women have cracked the glass ceiling, including Gwynne Shotwell, president and chief operating officer of SpaceX. But unlike their male counterparts, they usually don't have stay-at-home spouses who do all the household management and childcare.

• **"He allows her, in Church as well as State, but a subordinate position . . ."** Most conservative religions adamantly refuse to open the door to women's leadership. We all know who they are. However, female pastors, priests, and rabbis in progressive congregations usually don't honor the Seneca Falls visionaries—or any other feminists.

• **"He has created a false public sentiment, by giving to the world a different code of morals for men and women."** Very few people expect women to be virgins on their wedding night nowadays. Even though they preach premarital abstinence for both women and men, Catholic and conservative evangelical leaders have been shocked to find out that many members of their churches are cohabiting. [9]

But other aspects of the double standard have endured without a dent. In 1848, women were told to look the other way when their husbands and sons collected "dirty drawings and photographs." In 2024, many "relationship experts" give women the same advice when the men in their lives click on Pornhub because "it's just biology." If a man doesn't consume porn, he is either considered a hero or his masculinity is questioned. How much has *really* changed since 1848?

• But the most damning item in the declaration is the
one Sheryl Sandberg should have quoted in *Lean In*:
**"He has endeavored, in every way that he could, to
destroy her confidence in her own powers, to lessen
her self-respect, and to make her willing to lead a
dependent and abject life."**

The Declaration of Sentiments will continue to hold up a mirror to
American society for a long, long time. It should be studied in history
and political science classes as much as the brilliant, groundbreaking,
but imperfect document on which it is based: the Declaration of
Independence.

I know that the Declaration of Sentiments did not address
injustices to Black and immigrant women, which brings me to another
aspect of the suffragists' intellectual brilliance: the bracing insights of
Sojourner Truth, Ida B. Wells, Mary Church Terrell, Harriet Tubman,
Maud Sampson Williams, Juno Frankie Pierce, Jovita Idar, Andrea
and Teresa Villarreal, Mabel Ping-Hua Lee, and so many others on
the intersection of misogyny and racism—the double jeopardy—that
continues to challenge us to invoke our better angels.

As Mary Church Terrell said: "A white woman has only one
handicap to overcome—that of sex. I have two—both sex and race. . . .
Colored men have only one—that of race."

Amalfi Parker Elder and Patrice Tillery remind us, "Black women
have a long tradition of creating their own spaces where they can show up
as a whole person, and not just as a woman, or just as a Black person." [10]
In blatantly racist nineteenth and early twentieth century America,
Black women were forced to start their own suffrage organizations. They
boldly pushed the envelope and refused to be ignored within mainstream
suffrage organizations, knowing full well that there was almost no chance
that NAWSA would accept their groups even as auxiliary members.

In *The Vote*, there's a fascinating story about an encounter between
Carrie Chapman Catt and African American suffragists:

The six thousand members of the Northeastern Federation of Colored Women's Clubs, meanwhile, applied for membership in the National Association, fully expecting to be told that the timing was not advantageous. When Carrie Chapman Catt, through the National's secretary, begged them to withdraw the application for the sake of the amendment's passage, the Federation's president, Elizabeth Carter, readily agreed—on the condition that the National pledge to stand for the amendment as originally drawn, without modification. [11]

Catt steadfastly refused to support a "whites only" amendment, as stated in the "Why Many Say the Suffragists Were Not Racists" and "Carrie On" sections of this book.

Black, Hispanic, Asian, and Native American suffragists were much more than the conscience of the movement. From the get-go, they analyzed the intersections and educated us about their complexities. Women of color have a different experience of sexism than white women, and a different experience of racism than the men of their racial group. Indeed, when people mention the racism directed at Kamala Harris and Ketanji Brown Jackson but ignore the sexism, I tell them, "Just say misogynoir."

When I was researching Texas suffragists, I discovered Andrea and Teresa Villarreal, two sisters who in 1909 published one of Texas's first feminist newspapers, La Mujer Moderna. [12] Excited about the possibility of putting this information in the National Votes for Women Trail database, I tried very hard to find a copy of the newspaper. I also tried to find out if the building where it was produced still exists. But I found nothing. I called the Blagg-Huey Library at Texas Woman's University, and the special collections librarian was as frustrated as I was.

My experience with the Villarreal sisters showed me once again the precariousness of all women's history, especially the history of women of color, and why it is crucial to preserve it, promote it, and fight for it.

It cannot be said too often. Suffragists of all races and classes made us expand our horizons because they were extraordinary visionaries. And vision leads to the next trait that made the suffragists great.

They Were Phenomenal Innovators

It took a lot of marketing savvy over the course of more than seventy years to turn an almost forbidden idea into an institution as taken for granted as baseball and apple pie. Indeed, suffragists skillfully used baseball games as places for activism. They lobbied at the games ("Make a home run for suffrage") and highlighted baseball players who supported "votes for my mom, my sisters, my daughter, and my wife." Trixie Friganza, an actor and suffragist, inspired the popular song "Take Me Out to the Ballgame." [13]

But the suffragists' greatest innovations were the magnificent protest marches and examples of heterosexual marriages that started to pave the way towards fairness and equity. They also helped pave the way towards acceptance of same-sex marriages. When I saw the beautiful pictures of the legendary 1913 Suffrage Parade, I didn't realize how much I was viewing them through twenty-first century eyes until I watched the PBS series *The Vote*.

As historian J. D. Zahniser reminded us, for those who are constantly exposed to marches at the nation's capital, it's hard to believe that national protests in Washington were almost nonexistent in 1913. [14] Mary Walton noted that the parade wasn't just women in white dresses marching with "Votes for Women" signs:

> It was a narrative of women's progress, from pioneer days all the way up to present day. The present day consisted of phalanxes of women marching by profession. You had your librarians. You had your

teachers. You had your nurses. The message was, "This is the contribution that women make to society." [15]

Alice Paul, as the main architect of the parade, got plenty of on-the-job training in the fine art of organizing protest marches when she lived in England and participated in suffrage marches led by Emmeline Pankhurst. But she still put her distinct stamp on the parade in Washington and was a virtuoso at creating a media sensation. The parade overshadowed the inauguration of the president of the United States.

The powerful White House protests, led by Alice Paul, Lucy Burns, and the Silent Sentinels, were another great innovation. As historian Colonel Beth Behn noted, "For women to stand at the gates of the White House and demand attention from the president, to demand rights, is stepping far outside of social norms for that time." [16] Susan Ware noted:

> There had been picket lines in the labor movement for years. It's not a tactic that they invented. But applying it to suffrage and using the White House and specifically its occupant, Woodrow Wilson, as the target, was something entirely new. It was a brilliant way of upping the ante. [17]

Alice Paul, Lucy Burns, and the Silent Sentinels were consummate directors of political theater. Arguably, the Prison Special was even more spectacular than the White House protests. In 1919, they launched a train tour, "From Prison to People," throughout the United States. They wore their prison uniforms to publicize their horrendous treatment as prisoners and to keep Congress from dragging its feet on the women's suffrage amendment. In June 1919, just three months after the conclusion of the Prison Special, Congress finally passed the Nineteenth Amendment.

I once met a woman who took a college-level course on political protests. I asked her how much attention the teacher gave to the suffrage protests. "Almost none," this student said, and admitted that she had never complained. I told her that she has a right to demand her money back and give the teacher a negative review. There is no valid excuse to trivialize those tremendous contributions to the fine art of political protests, especially when it's *de rigueur* to protest at the White House nowadays.

When I was watching *The Vote*, the narrators quoted Woodrow Wilson's patriarchal question, "Who is going to [make the home] if the women don't?"[18] And that's when I realized that the suffragists were underrated innovators in another crucial area—family life. They showed the world that a marriage is not going to fall apart if—gasp!—husbands do housework and childcare, and wives are out in the world doing activism.

The most misogynistic—and effective—anti-suffrage cartoons were those of hapless husbands whose wives were out campaigning for voting rights. However, when Edna Buckman Kearns was doing suffrage activism, her husband Wilmer Kearns competently managed the household.[19] Ida B. Wells and her husband, lawyer and journalist Ferdinand Barnett, worked together as a power couple—highly unusual for their time—and had four children. Lucy Stone and Henry Blackwell had an "anti-wedding" wedding in 1855, where she kept her name and they gave a speech renouncing the legal powers of husbands over wives.[20]

We don't state this other innovation nearly enough: the Boston marriage. This nineteenth century term describes a long-term relationship between two women who lived together and were financially independent of men. The Boston marriages of lesbian and bisexual women in the feminist movement paved the way for same-sex marriage to become legal in the twenty-first century.

Of course, innovative protests and marriages wouldn't have accomplished much if the leaders and marchers didn't have considerable political skill, which brings me to the next trait that made the suffragists great.

They Had Tremendous Political Acumen

It took subtle political skills in the Jim Crow era to steer the Nineteenth Amendment to victory. The beautiful roadside markers sponsored by the National Votes for Women Trail are loaded with stories about local suffragists showing their political sophistication. As Tennessee historian Carol Lynn Yellin said, "The suffragists were the greatest politicians the world has ever seen because they won the right to vote without having it."[21] As Coline Jenkins said:

> If you want to know about democracy, and the tools of democracy, then learn about the suffrage movement. This was warfare, and the suffragists used every single weapon available: petitions, lobbying, newspapers, speeches, marches—everything except the gun.[22]

It would be great if someone would write a self-help book for activists about the political techniques of suffragists and historical feminists, especially when a millennial acquaintance told me that when she delved into Carrie Chapman Catt's biography, she realized that she could apply Catt's tricks of the trade to her own environmental advocacy.

Indeed, when I started doing research on Dallas suffragist Nona Boren Mahoney, I was immediately struck by her great question to Sen. Barry Miller: "What will it take to convince you to change your mind on women's suffrage?"[23] That question was so on the mark that I used it in a voicemail to Sen. John Cornyn after the Uvalde mass shooting: "What will it take to convince you to change your mind on gun sense? What will it take to convince you to support commonsense gun control laws?" I don't know if my message had any impact, but he eventually played a major role in passing the Bipartisan Safer Communities Act.

The suffragists' political acumen was also shown in their adaptability to a country that was becoming more multiethnic and multireligious.

In the 1910s, the movement had come a long way from the 1848 Seneca Falls conference, when most attendees were Quakers, Wesleyan Methodists, Congregationalists, Presbyterians, and Episcopalians of English, Scottish, and Dutch descent. [24]

Imprisoned suffragists were Catholic, Protestant, Jewish, and secularist, with ancestors from England, Scotland, Ireland, France, Switzerland, the Netherlands, Germany, Sweden, Norway, Poland, Russia, Ukraine, and Armenia. [25]

Early twentieth-century suffragists lived in a time when many white Americans lived in ethnic neighborhoods and worshipped in ethnic churches and synagogues, especially in the Midwest and the Northeast; when stupid and often demeaning ethnic jokes were not just tolerated but encouraged; when people were strongly encouraged to marry within their own ethnic group and religion; and when stage and movie stars were often forced to anglicize their names. John Krajewski would never have been able to keep his own name if he had made movies in 1919. It's quite remarkable that both NAWSA and NWP had built a community with suffragists from so many ethnic groups and religions.

The more I learn about the suffragists' political skills, the more it irritates me when people say, "Women were *given* the vote." But that irritation morphs into anger when reminded of their immense sacrifices.

They Were Heroic

I do not believe in heroes or heroines, but I have no problem acknowledging that people can perform heroic acts. Mabel Ping-Hua Lee's suffrage leadership when Chinese immigrants couldn't become American citizens was a true act of heroism—of putting others first.

The heroism of Maud Sampson Williams, Ida B. Wells, Mary Church Terrell, Harriet Tubman, Sojourner Truth, Juno Frankie Pierce, and other Black suffragists who agitated for integration NOW must always be honored. They exemplified Dorothy Height's maxim, "If the time is not ripe, we have to ripen the time."

I say that as someone who is convinced that white suffragists were forced to play realpolitik and do not deserve to be pilloried. Painful but true: If the suffrage movement had been completely integrated, the Nineteenth Amendment would have been dead on arrival. Nevertheless, the times do not magically ripen by themselves. The groundwork must be laid, and Black suffragists did a heroic job.

Every women's history advocacy organization, including the National Women's History Alliance and the Lucy Burns Museum, needs to say point blank that the suffragists who went to prison and got tortured deserve as much honor as our heroic civil rights and military leaders. All of us need to proclaim that Alice Paul deserves as much recognition as Martin Luther King and Nelson Mandela.

Above all, we need to stop carping at Elizabeth Cady Stanton and say along with Joan Bradley Wages, former president and CEO of the National Women's History Museum:

> Make no mistake—the immensity of her contribution deserves more than a footnote. If our nation's ultimate creed is 'equality,' then she belongs on the same list as Abraham Lincoln, Martin Luther King Jr., Thomas Jefferson, and Frederick Douglass. [26]

Suffragists deserve the highest level of respect, and we are obliged to fight back when they don't get it. There seems to be no limit to the risks they took for our voting rights. I just found out that Nevada suffragists went into the mines by elevator, tunnel, ladder, and in buckets to talk to miners who were on shift. [27]

As Carrie Chapman Catt said so well,

> Women have suffered agony of soul which you never can comprehend, that you and your daughters might inherit political freedom. That vote has been costly. Prize it!

The vote is a power, a weapon of offense and defense, a
prayer. Use it intelligently, conscientiously, prayerfully.
Progress is calling to you to make no pause. Act![28]

And never let anyone trivialize the suffragists' brilliance and heroism.

A Sign of Hope
from Tennessee

My friend, Paula Casey, had invited me to the unveiling of
the Mattie Coleman National Votes for Women Trail marker in
Nashville, so I took a spur-of-the-moment road trip in the spring of
2023 to Tennessee. Because of my work schedule, I didn't have the
time to see any monuments in the eastern part of the state, and I
wasn't able to see every monument in Nashville. Nevertheless, I was
impressed with the fact that they had statues in Memphis, Nashville,
Clarksville, and Knoxville. I knew that the Tennessee suffrage statues
project had started in 1995, when this country was commemorating
the seventy-fifth anniversary of the Nineteenth Amendment, and
that it had taken immense organizational and fundraising efforts to
bring the project to fruition.

But as I was driving, I wondered, "Are they going to knock down
the suffrage movement in the descriptions next to the statues, just like
they did in Central Park? Will we get lectures on the suffs' flaws and
realpolitik when they unveil the Mattie Coleman marker? I don't want
to go through the Austin and Lucy Burns Museum experience again."
I had gotten so used to put-downs at suffragist memorials that I was
bracing myself for another disappointment.

However, as I was crossing the Mississippi River on the way to
Memphis, I saw a faint outline of the Equality Trailblazers Monument,
sculpted by Alan LeQuire, and got a glimmer of hope. When I walked
to the terrace behind the University of Memphis Cecil C. Humphreys

Figure 13: Memphis suffrage monument at night.

School of Law and saw the six busts and thirteen glass panels beautifully lit up at night, all I could say was, "Wow! Now that's a monument. This is a must-see for everyone who visits Memphis, even if they're not interested in the suffrage movement."

Unveiled in 2022, the monument is far from a last-minute, "Oops, we forgot about the Nineteenth Amendment Centennial, and we need to do something because a few feminists are barking" coverup. Thirteen great local activists—twelve women and one man—are represented on the panels. Each person has a glass panel with an engraved image, a quote, and a biography. In front of the panels are busts of five suffragists and one suffragent: Mary Church Terrell, Ida B. Wells, Marion Griffin, Charl Ormond Williams, and Reps. Lois DeBerry and Joe Hanover. [29]

I read each panel carefully and didn't find anything even close to the put-downs on the description next to the Women's Rights Pioneers Monument in Central Park or the descriptions in the Alice Paul Center for Gender Justice. There was no carping, no lecturing. The monument was intersectional without activists "waving it around like a slice-and-dice Ginsu knife," as Katha Pollitt would say. [30]

Seven panels honor local suffragists and one honors a suffragent: [31]

- **Lide Smith Meriwether** founded the Memphis Equal Rights Association in 1889 and was president of the Tennessee Equal Rights Association from 1897 to 1900.

- **Lulu Colyar Reese**, Memphis leader of the Ladies Hermitage Association, had a smoking salon at the Hermitage Hotel for women staying there during the ratification vote.

- **Ida B. Wells**, a pioneering anti-lynching activist and suffragist, started her journalism career in Memphis. She founded the Alpha Suffrage Club, and she integrated the 1913 NAWSA parade in Washington, DC. She co-founded the NAACP.

- **Mary Church Terrell**, a Memphis native, was the first president of the National Association of Colored Women (NACW) and co-founder of the NAACP. She picketed the White House with the NWP.

- **Alma Law** was the first woman to serve on the Shelby County Quarterly Court before it became the County Board of Commissioners.

- **Marion Griffin** was the first woman to practice law in the state of Tennessee. She was turned down to practice law by two judges, but she persuaded the state legislature to change the law.

- **Charl Ormond Williams** was a nationally recognized educator. Gov. Roberts was so impressed with her ability to bring factions together that he asked her to chair the Nineteenth Amendment ratification effort.

- **Joseph Hanover**, a state representative from Memphis, acted as the floor leader. He had to deal with death threats and anti-Semitic slurs as he skillfully kept pro-suffrage politicians together and enabled Harry Burn's last minute "yea" vote to push the Nineteenth Amendment to victory.

Five panels highlight local women whose careers were made possible by the Nineteenth Amendment: [32]

- **Frances Grant Loring**, co-founder of the Tennessee Lawyers Association for Women, was the only white woman to march with Martin Luther King during the sanitation strike.

- **Maxine Smith** was the executive director of the Memphis NAACP for over forty years.

- **Minerva Johnican** was the first Black female Shelby County commissioner and the first woman to serve as Shelby County Criminal Court clerk.

- **Happy Jones**, a major philanthropist, helped avert a second sanitation workers' strike.

- **Lois DeBerry** was the first woman to serve as speaker pro tempore of the Tennessee House of Representatives.

A unique aspect of the monument is that while it looks back, it also looks forward. To quote Paula Casey, "Public art is forever." [33] If anyone desecrates this monument or suggests that we tear it down, I am confident that Memphis women's history advocates will lead a social media tsunami around the world.

The next stop on my journey was the Jackson City Hall plaza, where I saw artist Wanda Stanfill's bust of Sue Shelton White.

I've always admired "Miss Sue" because she went to prison for my voting rights, toured the country in her uniform as part of the Prison Special, and was a staunch New Deal Democrat.

Since I have a classical music background, I could also relate to her because her mother was a piano teacher, and she had both Black and white students.

Stanfill's bust beautifully captured White's combination of friendliness and sophistication, and yes, she would pass the happy-hour test. I love the caption that she was "a West Tennessee woman who changed America."

However, the "Suffragist, Lawyer, Activist" description was too modest, especially when I walked across the street to the courthouse and saw the message in Figure 15.

Here we go again. The heroism of suffragists who went to prison is so underrated. Sue Shelton White also made a supreme sacrifice, and her prison term probably played a role in her death from cancer at age fifty-six.

In the future, she should be described as a "Heroic Suffragist, Trailblazing Attorney, New Deal Pioneer" because of her role as principal counsel of the Social Security Administration.

Nevertheless, as I drove to Nashville, I was starting to feel confident that Tennessee history advocates, unlike New Yorkers, New Jerseyans, and the Virginians at the Lucy Burns Museum, weren't going to tear down their suffragists. The expansive Tennessee Woman Suffrage Monument near the Parthenon at Centennial Park looked different from Alan LeQuire's other suffrage monuments, but it had the same framework as the one in Memphis: Honor the past and show how it impacts the present.

The Nashville monument, unveiled in 2016, had statues of Anne Dallas Dudley, Abby Crawford Milton, Juno Frankie Pierce, Sue Shelton White, and Carrie Chapman Catt walking together in normal, everyday poses. Their biographies were on the panels around the

Figure 14 (left): Bust of Sue Shelton White at Jackson City Hall plaza in Jackson, Tennessee.
Photo by Jacque Hillman

Figure 15 (above): Message in the courtyard at the Madison County Courthouse.
Photo by Joanne Callahan

monument and there was no hint of condescension or finger-wagging. Sue Shelton White's time in prison was noted. The panels also had sculpted portraits of current local female political leaders from both parties, and it said that the Nineteenth Amendment changed America.

However, as Paula Casey drove me to Meharry Medical College for the unveiling of the Mattie Coleman marker, I thought, "Brace yourself. We'll probably get a lecture about the limitations of the Women's Suffrage Movement."

To my relief, none of the speakers scolded the suffragists for not being twenty-first century intersectional. Paula gave one of the speeches, and she rightly said that the vote was not given to women.

Nevertheless, all the speakers were too modest about Mattie Coleman's accomplishments, and they could have lauded her more without slipping into idolatry. They acknowledged her pioneering as a suffragist and as a doctor and dentist, but they should have also talked about her Christian feminism. To quote Linda T. Wynn:

A trailblazer, Dr. Mattie E. Coleman cleared the path
for Black women not only in the medical profession
but also in the male-dominated sanctuary of the Black
church and society in general. [34]

After the Coleman marker ceremony, Paula showed me Anne
Dallas Dudley Park and drove me around Anne Dallas Dudley
Boulevard, named after the witty and charismatic Nashville suffrage
leader who was beautiful enough to be a silent movie star. All I could
think was, "If only we had streets and parks named after great local and
national suffragists in every state in America."

Paula later took me to the magnificent Hermitage Hotel and raved
about its cocktails named after local suffragists. I listened politely but
thought, "This has to be a joke."

Cocktails for suffragists? Really? Alcoholic beverages named after
activists often aligned with the temperance movement? Perhaps they
were really mocktails—updated versions of the Shirley Temple. But
when I looked at the suffrage cocktails menu, it was the real deal. And
when I had the Sue and the Carrie, trust me, they were real drinks.
And darned good ones. I laughed at their cocktail for anti-suffragist
Josephine Pearson ("Resolute, Overzealous, Old-Fashioned") and
my only complaint was that they didn't have a cocktail for Joseph
Hanover—with kosher wine.

It's fair to ask whether it is historically respectful to have cocktails
for suffragists. But as far as I know, none of the suffs on the list were
complaining when Prohibition was repealed. I wouldn't be surprised
if several were members of Pauline Sabin's Women's Organization
for National Prohibition Reform. Political decisions have always
been made in bars, even during Prohibition. We don't know if the
suffs imbibed, but it's safe to bet that both the suffragents and their
retrograde "brothers" didn't confine themselves to iced tea and
lemonade. The Hermitage even had a secret Jack Daniels Suite that
wooed and boozed lawmakers to say "no" to votes for women. [35]

Photos by Joanne M. Callahan

Figure 16: Tennessee Woman Suffrage Monument in Nashville.

Figure 17: National Votes for Women Trail marker for Dr. Mattie Coleman, Meharry Medical College.

However, the Hermitage doesn't just honor its suffragists with cocktails like those listed in the menu shown on the next page. In the main reception area, there is a room full of suffrage swag, cartoons, and other memorabilia from those wild and crazy "war of the roses" days in Nashville, when suffragents wore yellow boutonnieres and antis wore red. The Hermitage, which has attracted superstars from around the world, could have easily stuck to the conventional and filled that room with autographed glamour shots of Charlie Chaplin, Babe Ruth, Amelia Earhart, Greta Garbo, President Kennedy, Aretha Franklin, and so many other legends, but I was very happy that they chose to honor the suffragists who triumphed over the Nineteenth Amendment during its treacherous last mile. I wish other hotels would do the same.

As far as I'm concerned, Tennessee has done the best job of honoring its suffragists (and yes, it could do more). I am especially impressed with the fact that Tennessee women's history advocates and media quietly refused to join in the trashing of white suffragists during the Nineteenth Amendment Centennial.

However, since Tennessee is a deep red state with Marsha Blackburn, a conservative anti-feminist Republican, in the Senate, people have asked me, "Was it worth it to spend all that time and money on suffrage history?"

My response has usually been, "You're asking if it was worth it for conservative Tennessee to honor its suffragists. However, I have never heard you question whether it's worth it for Memphis to have a National Civil Rights Museum even though Tennessee has never had a Black senator." They usually change the subject.

The Tennessee example should compel us to ask the question, "When will we get a set of impressive suffrage memorials in California, Illinois, Washington, and other blue states with a long history of progressive female political leaders? And when are we going to get a set of suffrage memorials in Texas, a state with a political culture so like the one in Tennessee?"

It wouldn't be much of a sacrifice for female Silicon Valley and Hollywood billionaires and their male allies to sponsor statues in Sacramento, San Francisco, Los Angeles, and San Diego.

As we go forward, Tennessee suffrage history advocates need to use the state's memorials as a stepping stone to advocate for Women's Equality Day to become a federal holiday, to improve our history textbooks, and to push for suffragists to get the Presidential Medal of Freedom. Advocates need to keep "ripening the times" and whetting people's appetite.

Indeed, when I found out about Prost, Mathilde!—a beer in honor of the great Mathilde Giesler Anneke, a Prussian refugee who settled in Milwaukee and became an abolitionist and suffragist leader who worked with Elizabeth Cady Stanton and Susan B. Anthony—I wondered if the brewers got the idea from the Hermitage suffrage cocktails.[36]

Figure 18: The Hermitage Hotel's suffrage cocktails are named after Tennessee activists.

SUFFRAGE COCKTAILS

THE ABBY 16
Enthusiastic • Tactful • Charming
Tito's, Sparkling Rose, Agave, Lime

THE ANNE 17
Charismatic • Sophisticated • Savvy
*Ford's Sloe Gin, Prosecco,
Chartreuse Herbal Syrup, Lemon*

THE CARRIE 20
Robust • Bold • Staunch
*Jack Daniel's Single Barrel, Chambord,
Holiday Syrup, Chocolate Bitters*

THE CATHERINE 17
Steadfast • Rational • Astute
*Diplomatico Reserva Rum,
Salted Caramel, Walnut Bitters*

THE FRANKIE 17
Leader • Educator • Politician
*Herradura Anejo, Watermelon Spice,
Ancho Reyes, Lime*

THE JOSEPHINE 16
Overzealous • Old Fashioned •
Resolute
*Herradura Reposado, Green Chartreuse,
Maraschino, Lemon*

THE SUE 16
Witty • Unconventional • Radical
*Gentleman Jack Bourbon, Falernum,
Coconut, Pineapple, Lime*

THE TIEBREAKER 17
Courageous • Honest • Patriotic
*Woodford Bourbon,
Amaro Montenegro, Ginger, Lemon*

The creators of Prost, Mathilde! are probably not aware of those great drinks, but I do believe in serendipity. Perhaps the Tennessee example will slowly catch on and suffragists in all states, especially the ones that ratified the amendment, will finally get the respect they deserve.

Standing Up
to Susan B. Anthony Pro-Life America

On January 14, 2017, *Saturday Night Live* surprised us with a skit about a group of young female tourists who visited the Susan B. Anthony House in Rochester and made the legendary suffragist come back to life by uttering a magic formula. After a lot of silly dialogue between the shallow visitors and Miss Anthony, the great activist ended the skit with the shocking punchline, "Abortion is murder."[37]

Not surprisingly, anti-abortion activists were elated and most of the audience was confused. Susan B. Anthony, an anti-abortion activist? Is this true? Or is this just a typical SNL snark designed to get a rise out of audiences?

In contrast to the silence after the Brent Staples bombshells about white suffragists and racism, Susan B. Anthony scholars and other suffrage historians immediately fired back and worked very hard to set the record straight. Deborah L. Hughes, president and CEO of the National Susan B. Anthony Museum & House, went on the Rochester NBC TV station to tell the world that the famous activist was not involved in the abortion issue and that anti-abortion activists are misinterpreting the few statements she made on the topic. Indeed, Hughes said that Anthony didn't even write one of the statements that anti-abortion activists attributed to her.[38] On the museum website, Victoria Brzustowicz, a member of the museum leadership team, responded to the numerous calls the museum got after the skit:

> We received many inquiries about her position in regard to abortion when Anthony was featured in a skit on *Saturday Night Live!* Because the set of the NBC skit included a remarkable likeness of the front parlor of 17 Madison Street AND named the Susan B. Anthony House, audiences assumed that we had been consulted on the contents. Actually, we had no idea that this skit was in the works.[39]

Brzustowicz directed readers to Harper Ward's detailed and concise "Misrepresenting Susan B. Anthony on Abortion" on the museum website.[40]

The dispute over Susan B. Anthony's views on abortion has been happening since 1989 and it's easy to find numerous online articles about it. Although evidence of Anthony's true view on abortion is flimsy at best, the durability of the Susan B. Anthony Pro-Life America political action committee, founded in 1993, provides strong evidence that the myth of Anthony as an anti-abortion activist has gained immense traction among conservatives and organizations like Feminists for Life.

But it hasn't convinced most moderates and progressives, because Susan B. Anthony scholars have provided such consistent opposition. In my presentations about the Women's Suffrage Movement, nobody has ever asked me about the abortion issue. Some older people still ask about Prohibition, and racism is a prominent question among all age groups, but never abortion.

Because Susan B. Anthony scholars have relentlessly pushed back on the anti-abortion myth, they have forced the media to report both sides of the issue. In Caroline Kitchener's *Washington Post* article, "Was Susan B. Anthony Antiabortion? Two Sides Are Dueling over the Answer—and the Definition of Feminism," she describes the three sources of the dispute.

In the *Revolution*, a newspaper managed by Elizabeth Cady Stanton and Susan B. Anthony, several people wrote articles on a wide variety of issues. There were articles that opposed abortion, and they are signed by "A." Anti-abortion activists claim that the "A" stands for Susan B. Anthony. However, Lynn Sherr, author of *Failure Is Impossible: Susan B. Anthony in Her Own Words*, doesn't buy it. "I have read every speech Anthony ever made. I have never seen her sign with the letter A. Period," Sherr said.[41] Ann Gordon says that on the few occasions when Anthony wrote articles for the *Revolution*, she signed them with SBA.[42]

Kitchener reports that in a speech on social purity in 1895, Anthony includes abortion in a list of societal ills, along with wife murders and infanticides. She also reports that Anthony referenced abortion in an 1876 diary entry about her sister-in-law, who aborted a pregnancy at home and was bedridden for days afterward. Anthony wrote that "she will rue the day she forces nature."[43]

Activists on all sides of the abortion issue will debate what Anthony meant by "she will rue the day she forces nature" until the end of time, but *there is absolutely no evidence that she did any activism on any abortion law*. She was completely silent about the Comstock Act of 1873, the law that made abortion illegal in this country.

And yet some visitors to the Susan B. Anthony House in Rochester still ask whether she was pro-life or pro-choice.

"It's like asking, 'Did George Washington drive a Maserati?' " Hughes joked.[44]

Hughes admits that she supports abortion rights: "I wish I could use my platform, but that would not be appropriate because it's not what Susan said."[45]

As someone who visited the Susan B. Anthony House in 2015, I can attest that the guides never talked about abortion, and nobody asked about it. I have not toured the Susan B. Anthony Birthplace Museum in Adams, Massachusetts, which has a display on the abortion issue. But on my next trip to New England, I will visit it and will draw my own conclusions about whether it really tells the whole story about Anthony or whether it is anti-abortion propaganda.[46]

As I reflect on suffragists and the abortion issue, I think of another controversy about a nineteenth century superstar: the theory that Abraham Lincoln was gay, as asserted in the controversial documentary *Lover of Men: The Untold History of Abraham Lincoln*. And I think of a claim consistently made by conservatives despite evidence to the contrary: Martin Luther King would have opposed affirmative action. However, why haven't activists formed Abraham Lincoln LGBTIQ+ America? Why haven't anti-DEI activists named one of their lobbying groups after Martin Luther King? Because they know it would be political suicide. Historians and the public would not stand for it. [47]

When Susan B. Anthony Pro-Life America started, there was controversy, but it didn't weaken the anti-abortion movement. Could the double standard have something to do with it? In a previous chapter, I complained that the Alice Paul Center for Gender Justice gets away with knocking down the brilliant, heroic suffragist/feminist while benefitting from her legacy—and her gorgeous family home. I have recently discovered the Abigail Adams Institute, a conservative group in the Harvard area, which is doing nothing to publicize the accomplishments of "Mrs. President" herself. But nobody is calling out the group for just using her name. We need to be extra vigilant about the world exploiting female historic figures.

Even with these threats, there is good news about the Susan B. Anthony Museum and House. After all the beatings that "Aunt Susan" has taken over the past nine years, the museum is still open on Tuesday through Sunday and is now leading a Susan B. Inspires Me campaign, an exciting project to build an immersive, state-of-the art, multimedia history museum close to Anthony's house. [48] Her life was too big and her impact too powerful to be adequately portrayed within the cute little three-story house she shared with her sister, Mary.

This project has the potential to set the record straight on damaging controversies. I am confident that the expanded museum will push back against the notion that Anthony was involved in the abortion issue.

I also know that the expanded museum will not be overly modest about Anthony's achievements. The home page of the Susan B. Anthony Museum and House says, "This is the home of one of the world's great revolutionaries." The Susan B. Inspires Me campaign says, "Susan B. Anthony changed the world. You can, too."

But how will it handle the racism issue and threats from the cancel-culture crowd? A display on Anthony at the Smithsonian's National Museum of African American History and Culture perpetuates the double standard of history. Patronizing her as "a protégé of Frederick Douglass," it claimed that "like many of her white contemporaries, Anthony battled with her own preconceived notions on race."[49] The museum never talked about Douglass battling with preconceived notions on women.

Ann Gordon's powerful video *Was Susan B. Anthony a Racist?* hints that the expanded museum will take an approach like John Blake's "Did Black Lives Matter to Abraham Lincoln? It's Complicated."[50] Linda Lopata's "If Susan B. Anthony Was a Racist" has strong words for those who refuse to grow up and acknowledge the complexities:

> At the time, Susan B. Anthony was almost universally reviled for her anti-racist views. White historians, to prove their anti-racist bonafides, have often ignored this fact, by taking her quotes out of context. Other white historians have focused entirely on Susan B. Anthony's anti-slavery work and close relationships with Black women, but ignored her willingness to work with racist suffragists. *It is as if she is a proxy for our own struggle with racism.*[51]

When I first listened to Gordon's video and read Lopata's article in 2020, I thought they were too academic and polite to deal with the vicious attacks on Anthony. But their detailed, nuanced approach in a great multimedia museum could have a powerful impact and make visitors realize that they have the same attitude as Myriam Miedzian: "The shaming must stop."[52]

Carrie On

Can a great American who didn't do sexy activism make the cut in the twenty-first century?

Carrie Chapman Catt didn't have the glamour of Inez Milholland, and she wasn't a badass like Alice Paul and the Silent Sentinels. The contemporary American media, with its intense focus on seductive visuals and sensationalist political theater, doesn't know what to make of her. *Iron Jawed Angels* made her look like a wealthy, conservative woman who did safe, ladylike activism that didn't make much of a difference. As I said before, *Suffs* treated her much better, but the musical still didn't catch what made her great.

When Alice Paul got canceled at the University of Pennsylvania in 2021, I thought, "Brace yourself. Catt Hall at Iowa State is next." Surely enough, the fractious Rename Catt Hall campaign that started on September 29, 1995, got reignited by the murder of George Floyd.

I wanted to get involved in a movement to defend Catt, especially after reading several vicious attacks in the *Iowa State Daily*, but since I wasn't part of the Iowa State community, I didn't know what to do. So I kept searching the Internet and found a collection of superb comments by Karen M. Kedrowski, director of the Carrie Chapman Catt Center for Women and Politics:

> I don't know of any rights movement that got criticized more for what it *didn't* accomplish than women's suffrage . . . The suffrage movement is often maligned because it was led primarily by educated, white, middle-class and wealthy women, as if the achievements of these people are not important . . . [53]

She made perceptive comments on the dispute between Susan B. Anthony and Frederick Douglass after the Civil War and how it carries over to the twenty-first century:

Susan B. Anthony was furious about the Fifteenth Amendment not including women. Many suffragists supported including women in the Fifteenth Amendment, but the idea was dropped for practical political reasons . . . "it's the Black man's turn." Frederick Douglass spoke about Black men, but Black women were left out of the conversation. . . .

Douglass's argument and others seem to imply that racism is a graver sin than sexism. We even see this today. The way our courts look at racial discrimination falls under the judicial principle of strict scrutiny, but sexism falls under intermediate scrutiny. Strict scrutiny places the burden on the defendant while intermediate scrutiny places the burden on the plaintiff. [54]

And she weighed in on racism:

There's a widely held belief that the suffrage movement was a social movement by and for white women. That's not true. There were many African American women working for suffrage nationwide and in Iowa, and the Nineteenth Amendment is not limited to white women. [55]

I immediately called Kedrowski and asked her what I as an outsider could do to help save Catt Hall. She told me that in 2020, Iowa State had developed a policy on removing names from university buildings. [56] After it had been adopted, students, staff, and alumni submitted several requests about Catt Hall. Because of all the controversy, a committee to review requests to rename Catt Hall had been formed.

The committee was interviewing people on all sides of the argument; however, committee members were selected partly because they were all neutral and had never made a statement about the controversial suffragist. The university had hired a research firm, History Associates Inc., to find every statement Catt had made on race and supply historical context.

When I heard those facts, I looked upward and thought, "University bureaucracy. They'll probably decide in the year 3027." Kedrowski acknowledged that the review process is long and laborious, but she said that after the initial review was complete, the public, including outsiders like me, could send comments. And then, the committee would make a final decision.

When I first heard about the review committee, I was not optimistic. The pandemic had shifted everyone's priorities, the cancel culture was still going strong, and I had heard very little about the Catt Hall controversy from the women's history community. But on August 25, 2023, the committee posted its initial report online and provided a comment form. [57] It had voted, nine to six, to retain the name. [58] I was relieved that a majority had voted in favor. But it was only 60 percent. I sent the report to Paula Casey and my comments to the committee. I was happier when the committee, in its final tally, voted eleven to four, a 73 percent majority, to "Carrie On" in November 2023. [59]

So what was the secret sauce that kept the Catt Hall name intact and that increased the percentage of "yes" votes in the final tally? In a nutshell: facts, balance, and maturity. The committee examined the complete picture of Catt's accomplishments, mistakes, and complexities and didn't indulge in presentism.

The report gave several little-known examples of Catt standing up to racism: her numerous speeches; her refusal to support a whites-only suffrage amendment; her suffrage activism for all women in South America, Europe, the Middle East, Africa, and Asia; her friendship with Mary Church Terrell; her defense of French Black soldiers falsely accused after WWI of crimes against German women; her strong anti-Nazi activism; her analysis of the causes of war; and her coruscating takedown of the Ku Klux Klan: [60]

The education of public opinion, which is the only real sovereign we know in this country, is endangered by these pillow and sheet maskers. Come out in the open, Mr. Kluxer. If you want to make a political war on any man or body of men, do it, but meet your opponents in the open field like brave Americans, and not behind an oath and a pillow case. [61]

The report didn't shy away from the hard stuff. Concerning her nativism and xenophobia, Catt herself said, "Once I was a regular jingo . . . I thought America had a monopoly on all that stands for progress, but I had a sad awakening." [62] Catt started out as a provincial American but ended up a cosmopolitan citizen of the world who never looked down on her Iowa roots.

But the killer is Catt's oft-quoted, "White supremacy will be strengthened, not weakened, by woman suffrage." [63] The report showed that before anyone can analyze what she really meant by that statement, we need to learn more about Catt's approach to life and politics. Catt lived in a blatantly racist society with severely limited choices for suffragists. She accepted the fact that sometimes, we need to do realpolitik. As she said in her 1921 commencement speech at Iowa State:

A single vote means nothing—a block of votes means much. Therefore you must learn to work with others. I believe that it is the hardest lesson that any human being ever has to learn . . . It means that you must concede, you must compromise, you must ever respect the opinions of others. Stand together. [64]

Catt practiced what she preached. To gain traction on the women's suffrage amendment, she compromised her pacifist views when the United States entered WWI and got tremendous flak from peace activists. Catt and other suffragists knew that the window for passing an amendment, especially one that prioritizes women's rights, doesn't last forever. As suffrage historian Colonel Beth Behn pointed out, "There was a sense of time and urgency, and I think Catt sensed that. And if we look outside the boundaries of the United States, you can see women in Great Britain aren't enfranchised until 1928 . . ." [65]

So where does the report leave Catt's comments about white supremacy? It says that white suffragists, when dealing with Southern politicians, often used the stats-and-numbers technique to defuse arguments about race:

> "White supremacy," in this case, referenced a simple statistical fact: White men and women outnumbered Black men and women in most of the South [by half a million in the fifteen states south of the Mason-Dixon line]. Therefore, the suffragists argued, if American women gained the ballot, white voters would easily outnumber Black voters, thus establishing "white supremacy." [66]

In the 1917 book *Woman Suffrage by Federal Constitutional Amendment,* Catt wrote the chapter "Objections to the Federal Amendment" and yes, she said, "White supremacy will be strengthened, not weakened, by women's suffrage." Some believe that Catt is appealing to racism, but others insist it is one sentence in a book chapter in which Catt catalogs the multiple objections to suffrage made by Southern politicians and then refutes them. In the book, she concludes:

> Ridiculous as this list of objections may appear, each is supported earnestly by a considerable group, and collectively they furnish the basis of opposition to woman suffrage in and out of Congress. The answer to one is the answer to all. Government by 'the people' is

expedient or it is not. If it is expedient, then obviously
all the people must be included. [67]

As a twenty-first century woman, it is hard for me to wrap my brain around the political tactic of acting like white supremacy just means there are more whites than Blacks. But if I was a suffragist and had to deal with Southern politicians, I don't think I or anyone else could have done a better job of playing realpolitik.

As I have said before, one of the most encouraging aspects of the Catt Hall controversy was that the final tally of "Carrie On" votes increased from 60 percent to 73 percent. Since the committee members didn't talk to the public about their votes, we can't say for certain why the percentage increased. However, after reading all the comments, I have a few theories.

Those who called Catt a racist kept repeating her "white supremacy will be strengthened" comment, but they never responded to the report's interpretation of it. They didn't even say, "What a crock of s---. I am not convinced." They had no respect for the difficulties of passing controversial legislation and how you had to play games with politicians. I agree with the numerous keep-the-name commenters who said the naysayers were immature. I would love to see how these ultra purists would have acted if they had to work with Southern legislators in the early twentieth century.

Several commenters filled in the gaps in the report by giving more examples of Catt standing up to racism, which may have convinced the two naysayers to change their votes:

> Even in her eighties, she was active, becoming a member of the Council Against Intolerance in America, a group formed to counteract the propaganda of racial and religious prejudice, which seeks to divide America in order to destroy it.
>
> —Jane Cox [68]

I have personally read the book chapter that refers to the white supremacy argument that was made by Southern male senators at the time and believe it to be in the context of a debate strategy, not one mired in racism.

—Maggie Roby[69]

To attain suffrage in New York in 1917, then the most populous and powerful state, she created a multi-generational, multiracial, cross-class coalition.

—Linda Duckworth[70]

Catt's work eventually redeemed her earlier writings—writings that seem to us to be racist. Throughout her career, political strategy seems to have trumped even her most strongly held principles, but the arc of her work bent eventually to peace, justice, and universal suffrage.

—Karen Agee[71]

Hitler probably put her on his "arrest" list.

—Joanne Callahan[72]

The Colorado referendum in 1893, where Catt traveled the state and organized scores of local pro-suffrage groups, enfranchised African American women as well as white women.

—Karen M. Kedrowski[73]

Kedrowski also provided statistics about African American women that should have been in the report:

The number of African American women enfranchised by the Nineteenth Amendment is significant.

According to the 1920 Census, about a half million African American women lived outside the states of the former Confederacy, which was about 25 percent of the African American female voting age population. We also know that many thousands of Black women, including thousands in the South, registered to vote in the 1920 election.

Between 1920 and 1960, millions of African Americans migrated to the Northeast and the Midwest in order to escape the double burdens of poverty and Jim Crow. According to the 1960 Census—the last Census before the Voting Rights Act of 1965— the African American female population over age twenty-one was about five million. Two million of these women, or 40 percent, lived outside the old Confederacy, and enjoyed full voting rights. [74]

The naysayers who changed their votes may have been impacted by numerous reminders that very few buildings at Iowa State are named after women and that society still views the male as the gold standard:

If not for her efforts, would we have a woman president of Iowa State University, a woman governor, a past woman secretary of agriculture, 80 percent plus women's enrollment in the College of Vet Medicine?
—Nancy Degner [75]

In the past seven years, our nation has experienced an incredible backlash against women . . . There has been a movement to discredit women who worked for the right to vote . . . It should be noted that the same people who argue that suffragists were racist do not also claim that the men who omitted women from the Fifteenth Amendment were sexist. "What's good for the goose is good for the gander."

— Carol Donovan [76]

But this was a truly remarkable woman and national leader of women—as close to a woman president as we've seen to that time—with far less baggage than most prominent men.

—Robert P. J. Cooney Jr. [77]

It's time to let another Catt out of the bag. Stop being so patronizing to this great Iowan.

—Joanne Callahan [78]

To those who think that every American on the planet now supports women's voting rights, two commenters, "Letter Down" and Connor Leitner, provided a reality check. They told the world that women's suffrage has ruined society. "Letter Down" even said that Catt must be rolling in her grave because of her "mistake." [79]

Nevertheless, my intuition tells me that the comments made by the leaders of the Tennessee suffrage statues and memorials project played the biggest role in changing the two naysayer votes. Paula Casey, Elizabeth Cave, Alan LeQuire, John Phillip Williams, Shirley Raines, William Haltom, and Jimmy Ogle provided powerful comments about the difference Catt made in Tennessee. They said she was a leader, not just a participant or a consultant. John Phillip Williams called her a field marshal and thought it was idiotic to cancel her. [80]

The Tennessee crowd lauded Catt's impact on Joseph Hanover, whom I chronicled in the section titled "Lauding Harry Burn While Ignoring Joseph Hanover."

As impressive as her work was in Tennessee, I wonder if we could have gotten even more "Carrie On" votes if the committee members had watched *Citizens at Last* and had seen the great advice on strategy that she gave Minnie Fisher Cunningham in Texas and how well she mentored her.

Nevertheless, I treated myself to a wonderful happy hour with friends when I saw the final eleven-to-four vote. In May 2024, I drove to Catt Hall from Dallas and took a day trip with Karen Kedrowski to the Carrie Chapman Catt Girlhood Home in Charles City. Both sites were lovely, and I wish I could have visited the Girlhood Home in the fall, when the apple trees are full. It felt almost like a fairy tale to wander through the countryside and reflect on a girl with immense leadership talent who grew up on a farm in rural Iowa and played a pivotal role in updating our Constitution and galvanizing Women's Suffrage Movements around the world. I was so impressed that I bought a brick that got set into the path leading to Catt's house.

However, like almost every suffragist site I have visited, Catt Hall and the Girlhood Home are much too modest about her talents and accomplishments. The Girlhood Home website says she was "A skilled political strategist . . . who helped secure for American women the right to vote."[81] Oh, please. Catt was an *outstanding* political strategist and organizer who led NAWSA, the largest women's suffrage organization in the United States, through its most productive years and played a leading role in securing American women's voting rights.

Like her mentor Susan B. Anthony, Catt's life was too big and her impact too powerful to be adequately portrayed within her pretty girlhood house and farm. A few days before I drove to Catt Hall, I visited the Woody Guthrie Center in Tulsa, a state-of-the-art, hagiographic museum with a sophisticated research center on Guthrie's music, a superb rendering of the 1930s "Dust Bowl" environmental disaster, and a cute touch screen of the great protest singer's travels.[82]

As I was touring Catt Hall, I thought, "Carrie Chapman Catt is ten times more worthy of a touch screen than Woody Guthrie. We need to see her travels around the world and the impact she had on women and men in all the countries she visited. We could see her riding in a horse and buggy, stagecoach, train, ocean liner, Zeppelin, and airplane. And we should see her driving a Model T. She experienced so much technological change in her lifetime." That touch screen needs to be in the State Historical Museum of Iowa, across the street from the Capitol.

If anyone is wondering why I didn't say that the touch screen should be in Catt Hall, it is because the state historical museum is more centrally located, and I don't want to incite the tiger. The Catt Hall controversy will continue as long as we have a double standard of history.

Indeed, Carrie Chapman Catt is missing from Jane DeDecker's majestic *Every Word We Utter* prototype that inspired the campaign for the Women's Suffrage National Monument on the Capitol Mall. [83] That omission sends a powerful message: Your more than thirty years of women's suffrage activism, with a long list of outstanding accomplishments, will be forgotten. Is it any wonder that many women are reluctant to do feminist activism? DeDecker is on the design team for a suffrage statue scheduled to be unveiled on the Capitol Mall sometime in 2030 or 2031. As of this writing, nobody knows what the monument will look like, which gives us time to mount an organized fight for Catt.

It would be devastating if Anna Laymon, the president and CEO of the Women's Suffrage National Monument Foundation, did not insist that this consummate politician get the recognition she deserves. Laymon overcame stringent male opposition to putting the monument on the Mall and lobbied Congress and the executive branch in a way that would do Catt proud. [84]

I know that several people do not want Catt on the statue because she never gave the great Alice Paul credit for her phenomenal work. She and President Wilson kept Paul from participating in the Nineteenth Amendment signing ceremony. Yes, that was mean of her and Wilson, and one of the saddest aspects of the women's suffrage campaign was that Paul and Catt never reconciled. They never gave themselves a chance to get together for afternoon tea in the 1940s and have a few good laughs about the clueless politicians they had to work with.

But to paraphrase Bob Cooney, Catt had far less baggage and far less meanness than the numerous men who got idolized on the Mall. One of the anthems of the Nineteenth Amendment Centennial was "Hard Won, Not Done." The anthem applies not only to affirming women's voting rights but also to promoting women's history.

Preserving Catt Hall was a hard-won victory. But we still haven't completely taken the Catt out of the bag. As I said in my comments about Catt Hall:

> Multitudes of women and men of all races around the globe have benefitted immensely from her activism. It will probably take a Steven Spielberg movie to show the behind-the-scenes organizational skills that made her great—and help her finally get the respect she deserves in the twenty-first century.

In the age of Trump, we need people with Catt's consummate political skills. You don't have to do sexy activism to get noticed one hundred years after the fact, provided that your promoters don't retreat in the face of hostility or indifference. When Angela Lansbury died, I thought, "If only she had played Carrie Chapman Catt in a movie that understood what made her great." So let's continue to "Carrie On" and make sure she doesn't get trivialized and canceled. She and other suffragists gave so much. It's time to completely repay the debt.

CLAIMING SUFFRAGISTS' TRUE PLACE IN HISTORY

"Women's Equality Day is meaningless to most people, but that's not an accident."
Soraya Chemaly, journalist [1]

"If the time is not ripe, we have to ripen the time."
Dorothy Height, civil rights and feminist activist [2]

"Now we can begin."
Crystal Eastman, suffragist, 1920s ERA activist [3]

CHAPTER FOUR

A few months ago, I told a few women's history advocates that we need to rebrand Women's Equality Day and start a movement to make it a federal holiday. I also said that we need a campaign to make our American history textbooks do justice to the suffragists. I was irritated about doing women's history busy work that was going nowhere, and I was tired of educating people about great suffragists. As I have said so many times in this book, most of the memorials are patronizing. They seem to expect us to have a "gratitude attitude" and expect nothing more.

Not surprisingly, I got a lot of reasons for sticking to the status quo: It's a heavy lift; we're tired; we don't have the money; DEI is getting kicked out of universities and corporations; women's reproductive rights are under attack, and this issue is taking all my energy; it took us so long to get those memorials; history is a side issue; we're in the age of Trump. Most of these reasons are valid. However, my suggestions were valid, too. Treating women's history like it is a side issue sends a sexist message: Women don't matter; women are inferior to men; we should be happy with a few statues and pats on the head; it's not worth it to do feminist activism because your successes will get barely acknowledged by those who have benefitted.

As a middle-class lay activist and history buff with no connections to the rich and powerful, I don't have the means to start an organization or to change the ones that already exist. But you and I can place "the stubborn ounces of our weight"—as poet Bonaro Overstreet described the fight for social justice—on laying the groundwork for a coalition to happen in the future.[4] Dorothy Height gave us no excuses: If the time is not ripe, we must ripen the time—even in the age of Trump.

This section is focused on what we can do as individuals to "ripen the time" and help set the stage for a campaign to make the Women's Suffrage Movement take its rightful place in American history. And yes, it is the start of a heavy lift. It requires us to get out of our comfort zone, to make noise and be seen, regardless of our personality type. It dares us to make people feel uncomfortable. It challenges us to endure moments of loneliness and drudgery, and to risk losing friendships and the support of loved ones.[5] But those are the same things the suffragists had to tolerate, especially before the movement gained powerful momentum in the 1910s and became an irresistible force for change.

Nevertheless, suffragists also experienced moments of great joy during the time of ripening. They made friends with dynamic people who shared their convictions. They discovered talents they never thought they had. They learned new skills and gained more confidence. They got compliments from people who changed their viewpoints because of their activism. Above all, they did their part to move the mountain. Little by little, they finally got organizations that, despite their imperfections, had the punch and power to take the suffrage amendment to the finish line.

The same thing can happen to the suffrage history movement. As Crystal Eastman said after the Nineteenth Amendment was ratified and the ERA movement was about to be born, "Now we can begin."

Look in the Mirror

When I wrote my original outline for this book, I didn't think of having a "Look in the Mirror" section. I thought that a section on Faludi's theory of matricide would adequately address how so many women, including feminists, have internalized misogyny. But after having had so many experiences where women's history advocates "yes" me to death on the way our culture patronizes suffragists and then turn around and do the same thing, I realized I had to say, "Look in the mirror."

It is easy to find cognitive dissonance in articles about suffragists, especially with the statement, "Women were given/granted the vote." Elaine Weiss emphatically stated,

> And that active verb—win—is important: Women were not given the vote; they were not granted the vote. As one commentator so aptly describes it: "They took it." [6]

And yet, in that same article, Weiss said,

> In that summer of 1920, one last state was needed to ratify the Nineteenth Amendment to the US Constitution—*giving* all women, in every state, the right to vote in every election . . . [7]

I am not trying to imply that Weiss, a superb writer, is a bad person or a hypocrite. I'm just saying that she's human and needs to up her game. (And her copy editor needs to be more observant.) To those who claim that since many women were indifferent or against suffrage, it's OK to say, "Women were given the vote," I tell them, "OK, but be specific and say that *suffragists and their male allies* gave women the vote. Don't act like it was a gift from men or a supreme being."

We all need to look in the mirror and work on ourselves as we advocate for women's suffrage history. Some will make significant progress with the help of a good feminist therapist, but others may just need friends who tell them the truth and give them the time and space to work on their issues. As Cynthia Enloe said, "You need to have people around you who are differently feminist or more feminist than you are." [8]

Looking in the mirror and working on ourselves can easily become navel-gazing if we don't have clearly defined goals. One way to determine our progress is to examine how we react when someone gets defensive. As Alyson Krueger said,

> This is what we do as women. We say what we want, and the person we are telling it to gets defensive and pushes back, and then we apologize, and then we think what we want is greedy and wrong. [9]

Expecting suffragists to be treated as well as the "great men of history" is not greedy or wrong, but I have seen the poverty mentality so often in all types of women's groups that I can't resist quoting Jill Filipovic: "We've internalized a narrative of scarcity: we act as though we're fighting for crumbs." [10]

I know many women will say, "But we don't have the money, power, time, resources, you-name-it." I get that, but I have seen people think champagne when they barely have the money for beer. And it eventually pays off. They may not end up with *La Veuve Clicquot,* but they get a nice sparkling wine.

So when I told women's history advocates that we need to rebrand Women's Equality Day and start a movement to make it a federal holiday, and when I said that we need a campaign to make our American history textbooks do justice to the suffragists, how could they have avoided the poverty mentality and started ripening the times?

For starters, those who own women's suffrage websites could have corrected their overly modest comments about those great activists and they could have written an article on why Women's Equality Day needs to be a federal holiday.

For the *Her March to Democracy* podcast, which has wonderful content, they could have changed this overly modest statement:

> If you are a historian, history enthusiast, heritage tourist, or simply want to be inspired, listen to the stories of these remarkable and heroic activists who never wavered in their belief in democracy and the rule of law. [11]

To something like . . .

> Listen to the powerful, inspiring stories of these brilliant, heroic activists from every region in the country who never wavered in their belief in democracy, women's rights, and the rule of law.
>
> Share these great stories with your friends, your local history museum, and your senator and representative, especially during Women's History Month and Women's Equality Day. If you are a history teacher, use these stories in your classes. Make sure your students know about these great women.

These small changes won't automatically turn the suffs into household words, but they show that we are convinced they are good enough to be taken seriously in history textbooks. References to Women's History Month and Women's Equality Day—and hints to contact your senator and representative about them—convey that we view this podcast as a stepping stone to something greater.

Fight Back When Suffragists
Get Patronized, Attacked, or Ignored

Like practically every women's history advocate I know, I have gotten the cold shoulder when I have written letters complaining about a bad article or exhibit on the Women's Suffrage Movement. To paraphrase Carrie Chapman Catt, "A single letter means nothing—a block of letters means much."

So when are groups like the National Women's History Alliance going to send "fight back" emails to their sizable mailing lists and urge us to write a letter to a historian who trivializes the Women's Suffrage Movement? Feminist, environmental, and other social justice groups regularly send "fight back" emails to their mailing lists, but women's history groups are silent.

I know that when you deal with museums, historical commissions, universities, and government bureaucracies, you can't act like you're storming the Bastille. But remaining silent when people trash or patronize suffragists is just as damaging to the cause as physical violence. When women's history groups are silent, it tells me they subconsciously think suffragists are second-rate activists who don't deserve top-notch treatment.

All of us women have been socialized to meekly say "please" and think that if we just keep using positive reinforcement, we will get what we want. Several years ago, during a lecture at the Dallas Museum of Art on the French Revolution, the lecturer never mentioned the great pioneering feminist Olympe de Gouges and the women who petitioned the National Assembly for equal rights. The lecturer mentioned all the people who were "given their rights" in the early days of the revolution but said briefly that women weren't included.

During the question-and-answer period, I politely asked the lecturer why she never talked about Olympe de Gouges. To my surprise, several people in the Dallas audience, hardly a hotbed of feminism, were siding with me and saying in low tones, "Talk about her." The lecturer said she didn't have the time and then gave a lackluster description of the great activist. I learned my lesson. When you ask why women weren't included, lecturers can always give the lame excuse, "I didn't have time." Translation: Women's rights pioneers are trivial and they're not worth anyone's time. If I were to relive that moment, I would have said,

> I was offended when you never talked about the great Olympe de Gouges. *Le Monde* called her an exemplary eighteenth-century feminist and humanist and said that she should be honored in the Pantheon. [12] I agree.

> You should have said that de Gouges was an abolitionist who wrote the groundbreaking Declaration of the Rights of Women and of the Female Citizen in 1791, a momentous event in world history. Olympe de Gouges was guillotined for protesting the Reign of Terror. She was a constitutional monarchist strongly against revolutionaries resorting to violence. Neither a royalist nor a republican, she was one of the most heroic figures of the French Revolution.

> It was unprofessional and deeply sexist of you to ignore her. Without activists like Olympe de Gouges, you would have never been able to become a professor.

I would have also told the lecturer point-blank that rights are not gifts. There is no guarantee that the professor or audience would have heeded my words. I probably would have gotten a placating "Thank you for sharing" from the professor. But experience has shown me that there's a chance that someone in the audience will get it and start doing activism.

When I worked at Hewlett-Packard Enterprise, I did a presentation for the Women's Network on Elizabeth Cady Stanton's two hundredth birthday. I also talked about Alice Paul, Lucy Burns, and the Night of Terror. I emphasized that history classes need to treat the Women's Suffrage Movement as more than a footnote. To my surprise, the speaker who came after me encouraged audience members to "channel their inner Elizabeth Cady Stanton and Alice Paul." However, it was obvious that the conservatives in the group did not want to hear about these great feminists. I wondered if I had wasted my time. Months later, someone stopped me in the lobby. She said she loved my presentation and was starting to research the women's rights movement in her native China. Because of my speech, and other factors, an activist was born.

There is no reason women's history groups can't send "fight back" emails to supporters. I am not asking them to do it every month. But it would make a powerful statement if they did it during Women's History Month and around August 26 (Women's "Equality" Day). Yes, there will probably be a backlash. But it would tell the world that we are not going to suffer in silence when great women get a pat on the head and that we are going to make sure they are treated with the honor they deserve.

Resist When Second-Wave Feminists Get Trashed or Canceled

When I got the idea to write this book, I thought of including several sections on how feminists who did activism from the 1960s to the late 1970s were also getting trivialized. But time, money, and my frustration with so many people denigrating the first wave of feminism stopped me from doing it. So I decided to focus completely on American women's suffrage.

Nevertheless, I must express a few thoughts about the outstanding, albeit imperfect, activists who led one of the most thrilling periods in the history of the American women's movement, and how they're getting canceled. I know that some second wavers—mainly Gloria Steinem and the late Ruth Bader Ginsburg—continue to get accolades, but they are the exceptions. History warns us that they are not trash-proof. Carrie Chapman Catt and Inez Milholland got plenty of recognition during their lifetimes. But in the twenty-first century, they struggle to get the respect they deserve.

The Marxists and socialists I know have never forgiven Steinem for working for the Independent Research Service, an organization funded by the CIA, in the 1950s. [13] Shortly after she died in 2020, Ginsburg sometimes got flak for not retiring from the Supreme Court during the Obama years; telling activists they need to start over on the ERA; and not being intersectional enough. When a woman accused Ginsburg of "white feminism," I reminded her that after the Supreme Court gutted the enforcement provision of the Voting Rights Act, she told conservatives, "It is like throwing away your umbrella in a rainstorm because you are not getting wet." [14]

Second-wave feminists get trashed by pundits from all over the political spectrum, even though exceptional books have been written on these extraordinary activists' breathtaking achievements and devastating setbacks: Flora Davis' 1991 tome, *Moving the Mountain: The Women's Movement in America Since 1960*; Ruth Rosen's 2000 chronicle, *The World Split Open: How the Modern Women's Movement Changed America*; and Christine Stansell's 2011 opus, *The Feminist Promise: 1792 to the Present.*

But this literature has had very little impact on how pundits review history books. Reviews of Stephanie Coontz's popular *Marriage, a History: How Love Conquered Marriage* have been pretty silent about how she viewed the suffragist and feminist impact on "the conjugal bond." But when I read her book, I was pleasantly surprised to find that she acknowledged the eighteenth century pioneering not only of Olympe de Gouges, but Etta Palm d'Aelders of the Netherlands, Mary

Astell and Mary Wollstonecraft of Britain, Marquis de Condorcet of
France, and our own Abigail Adams. [15]

Coontz did a fine job of summarizing how both feminist activism
and its backlash have impacted marriage from the eighteenth to the
turn of the twenty-first century. I thank her profusely for including this
patriarchal (and misogynistic) quote from 1950s psychologist Clifford
Adams, a "marriage advisor," to *Ladies Home Journal*:

> The bride who wants to do her full job will plan from
> the start to create the kind of home her husband
> wants, and to do it with no more assistance from him
> than he willingly offers . . . And if hubby offers to dry
> the dishes, thank him for the favor, rather than regard
> it as your right. [16]

But Coontz should have juxtaposed it with this visionary 1920
quote from Crystal Eastman:

> It must be womanly as well as manly to earn your
> own living, to stand on your own feet. And it must be
> manly as well as womanly to know how to cook and
> sew and clean and take care of yourself in the ordinary
> exigencies of life. I need not add that the second part
> of this revolution will be more passionately resisted
> than the first . . . [17]

If Coontz had mentioned that Olympe de Gouges had been
executed, that would have been eloquent. It would have been helpful
if she had shown how Elizabeth Cady Stanton's visionary Declaration
of Sentiments holds up a mirror to twenty-first century heterosexual
marriage. I'm glad she admitted that most sex discrimination laws
were not enforced until the 1970s, and that enforcement was largely
because of pressure from women. [18] But her statement would have been

more powerful if she had acknowledged the pioneering of the National Organization for Women (NOW), which courageously took the lead in making the Equal Employment Opportunity Commission (EEOC) start enforcing those laws.

Coontz could have done much more to honor the suffragists and feminists who have worked so hard to make marriage less patriarchal and fairer to women. Nevertheless, she is much better than authors Sheryl WuDunn, Nicholas Kristof, and Fareed Zakaria at treating them with the respect they deserve.

WuDunn and Kristof's *Half the Sky: Turning Oppression into Opportunity for Women Worldwide* was an early twenty-first century blockbuster as both a book and a documentary. Like so many readers, I was deeply moved by its stories of women's monumental struggles in developing countries and inspired by their resilience and heroism. WuDunn and Kristof's insistence on data-driven, evidence-based solutions to complex problems was refreshing. I was cheering when they presented strong evidence of the benefits to children when mothers have "a purse of their own," to paraphrase Susan B. Anthony, and a strong, decisive voice in how the family money is managed. [19]

However, WuDunn and Kristof have been accused of a "white savior" mentality. Indeed, they viewed the British Abolitionist Movement as the ideal model for global women's rights activism and gave William Wilberforce, Thomas Clarkson, and the British navy—all white male leaders—the credit for its success. [20] They never introduced us to Mary Prince, a Black woman whose autobiography galvanized the anti-slavery movement. They never mentioned that slave revolts in Haiti helped turn the tide on British public opinion, and they were silent about British businesses buying cotton from American slave owners after slavery had been abolished.

When juxtaposed against the risks that WuDunn and Kristof have taken to write *Half the Sky*, their critics sound harsh. Still, they make valid points. But they should have also called them out for belittling American suffragists and feminists. To their credit, the authors quoted

Eve Ensler and Catharine MacKinnon in the introduction to a few chapters. They obviously respect Islamic feminists and Hillary Rodham Clinton and Marjorie Margolies-Mezvinsky.

They gave kudos to Equality Now, a global grassroots feminist organization headquartered in New York, and its founder, Jessica Neuwirth. But they called Equality Now an "advocacy organization" and dared not utter the "f" word. [21]

WuDunn and Kristof talked at length about why they now support the Nordic model, also known as the Swedish model, of dealing with prostitution, whereby sex workers/prostitutes are not arrested, but pimps and "johns" are penalized. [22] However, they never gave sociologist Kathleen Barry, author of the groundbreaking *Female Sexual Slavery* and *The Prostitution of Sexuality*, any credit for her superb pioneering activism. Nor did they give kudos to Swedish activists.

Likewise, when they lauded the Violence Against Women Act, guess who got all the credit? Senators Joe Biden and Richard Lugar. [23] WuDunn and Kristof ignored the fact that battered women's shelters and domestic violence task forces in groups like NOW paved the way for that landmark legislation.

When talking about American women's suffrage, they praised the immediate positive impact of local suffrage laws and the Nineteenth Amendment on public health and maternal mortality. But they turned around and said, "Women were given the vote" or "Women gained the vote." [24] We heard nothing about Alice Paul, Carrie Chapman Catt, and other brilliant, heroic suffragists, but when talking about the Civil Rights Movement, they treated Martin Luther King like Superman.

I know that the "f" word was completely taboo in 2009. But this book showed me why I started to rebel. When people avoid the "f" word, they often pander to people's prejudices. They either give credit for feminist successes to someone else (usually a man), or they use wimpy euphemisms, or they act like feminism had nothing to do with women's progress. Everyone agrees with WuDunn and Kristof that the American feminist movement is not perfect. But I was ticked off when they treated the imperfect British Abolitionist and American Civil Rights Movements as flawless role models.

WuDunn and Kristof need to get the "great man" theory of history out of their heads. Women in the developing world have already learned from the successes and setbacks of all Western social movements. Suffragists and feminists in the West and the developing world have always networked with each other. As Robin Morgan, author of the 1984 classic *Sisterhood Is Global: The International Women's Movement Anthology,* will tell you, the key to progress is for activists around the world to learn from each other and ditch the "savior" mentality.

In 2024, Fareed Zakaria worked the talk-show circuit with his book, *Age of Revolutions: Progress and Backlash from 1600 to the Present.* I was surprised when he said on *The Late Show with Stephen Colbert* that the biggest backlash in the twenty-first century is the backlash against women's progress. [25] Of course, I agreed with him, but I was stunned to hear this from Zakaria, who has never been known as an ally of the feminist movement.

So I bought his book and looked in the table of contents for words such as feminism, women's rights, and the like. I found nothing. Zakaria rightly says in *Age of Revolutions,* "Women's liberation may properly be called history's greatest social revolution," but he only devotes four pages to it. [26]

Zakaria is correct about the Industrial Revolution having a huge impact on the eighteenth and nineteenth century women's rights movement, but he thinks that industrialization set the movement in motion while I think it galvanized a movement that had already existed. Proto-feminist women had been writing about misogyny long before the steam engine had been invented.

Zakaria's statement about women's suffrage is unbelievably clueless: "Theirs was a reformist movement aimed mostly at extending voting rights to women, not at revolutionizing society." [27]

Has Zakaria ever read the Declaration of Sentiments? Has he ever studied the works of Elizabeth Cady Stanton, Sojourner Truth, Ida

B. Wells, Mary Church Terrell, Alice Paul, Susan B. Anthony, Carrie Chapman Catt, and so many other activists who viewed the vote as an essential first step in transforming society? Does he know that Crystal Eastman said "Now we can begin" *after* the Nineteenth Amendment was ratified? Does he know anything about the National Woman's Party, which started advocating for the ERA in 1923?

He seems to give "The Pill" and the Civil Rights Movement all the credit for starting the second wave of feminism:

> Yet suffrage had done little to change the lived reality of women across the country. As is so often the case, technological progress played a role in paving the way for social change. In 1957, the Food and Drug Administration approved the use of what would later become the first contraceptive pill. [28]

> The Civil Rights Movement served as a powerful catalyst for other social revolutions. From sit-ins to boycotts to marches, Black civil rights leaders had pioneered a model for other marginalized groups to voice their own grievances. Chief among those groups was the feminist movement. [29]

Zakaria ignores the fact that the birth control activism of Margaret Sanger and the financial underwriting of Katharine Dexter McCormick provided the impetus for the development of oral contraceptives. Activists don't just respond to technological change; sometimes, they drive it. I am not denying that the intellectual brilliance, political acumen, and heroism of the Civil Rights Movement galvanized the feminist movement. However, the spark also happened because there was so much misogyny in civil rights and New Left groups.

If Zakaria had studied the innovations of British and American suffragists, and if he had delved into the history of the women's movement from 1920 to 1966, he would have realized that feminism has always been its own movement. It is not a derivative. As Gandhi said when he visited London in 1909, "We have much to learn from the suffragettes." He believed that their willingness to suffer imprisonment or even death became an invincible "soul force." [30]

Zakaria lauds women's progress in higher education and the political arena, but he is silent about how second wavers brilliantly shattered the silence on violence against women; sexual harassment (a term they coined); the sexual politics of housework and childcare; oppressive standards of feminine beauty; sexist language; men's objectification of women; the double jeopardy that Black, Hispanic, Native and Asian American women face; homophobia; and so many other items. Zakaria doesn't seem to understand that one of the foundations of second-wave feminism is "the personal is political." To this day, millennial and zoomer feminists continue to build upon it with a strong intersectional focus.

Zakaria cites Simone de Beauvoir, but unfortunately he doesn't quote one of her most brilliant statements: "Humanity is male and man defines woman not in herself but in relation to himself; she is not considered an autonomous being." [31]

Most second-wave feminists stated plainly that the movement's goals are deeper than women getting equal pay, top jobs, and recognition for excellent work. They told the world to stop treating the male as the gold standard and start affirming women's full humanity.

To his credit, Zakaria doesn't have a problem with the "f" word and he doesn't point fingers when discussing anti-feminist backlash around the world. *Age of Revolutions* doesn't use male-centric language to describe the human race (i.e., mankind). If *Age of Revolutions* had been written fifty years ago, it probably would have reeked of phrases like "the rights of man" and "the brotherhood of all men."

I have read several reviews of *Age of Revolutions* and the only one that critiques his section on feminism is a customer review on Amazon. The reviewer's comments were somewhat similar to mine but she gives the book four stars. Zakaria is concerned about extremists dominating the landscape and his work is much more interesting than the typical dry-bones history textbook, but *Age of Revolutions* didn't deserve four stars.

During the past three years, a new crop of remarkable second-wave history books has been published: Rachel Shteir's 2023 *Betty Friedan: Magnificent Disrupter*; Katherine Turk's 2023 *The Women of NOW: How Feminists Built an Organization that Transformed America*; Clara Bingham's 2025 *The Movement: How Women's Liberation Transformed America 1963-1973*.

Second wavers haven't been forgotten at the movies. *On the Basis of Sex*, an episodic but enjoyable film about the young Ruth Bader Ginsburg, was released in 2018. It should have been a TV series. *Mrs. America*, released in 2020, caricatured Betty Friedan and was silent about anti-ERA corporate lobbyists, but it was still smart and stylish, with a splendid cast and that marvelous "A Fifth of Beethoven" opening credit sequence. The 2021 documentary *My Name Is Pauli Murray* was superb. It is tempting to think that more good books, movies, and TV shows will stop the trashing and that someday, we'll get halfway-decent accounts of second-wave activism in general history books.

But that's not going to happen unless we do history activism. Veteran Feminists of America (VFA), founded in 1992, is dedicated to honoring second-wave American feminists. It has a multitude of book reviews and stories about second wavers, both famous and unknown, on its website. But the group does not lead "fight back" email campaigns when pundits trash or trivialize these activists. It reviewed the Shteir, Turk, and Bingham books listed above, but it does not critique works like *Age of Revolutions, Marriage, a History,* or *Half the Sky*. It's strange that VFA takes such a subdued, ladylike approach to lauding such an outspoken group of activists.

Clara Bingham noted that there are many explanations for the beleaguered legacy of second-wave feminism. However, she doesn't go into much detail. I suspect that many are reluctant to defend second wavers because there is an excellent chance that someone is going to rant on Betty Friedan's mean streak, Kate Millett's mental health problems, Andrea Dworkin's "true" views on heterosexual intercourse, the rift between Alice Walker and her third-wave daughter, Rebecca, the divorce rate, and so on.

I can't help contrasting this reticence with an experience I had in a movie buffs' group several years ago. We were discussing *Shadowlands* and several evangelical Christians showed up for the conversation. Most were complementarian Republicans, but quite a few were egalitarian independents and Democrats. Regardless, they were all determined to defend C. S. Lewis. They unabashedly praised his superb writing skills, his dry British wit, and his unique gift for compelling people to examine their beliefs. "Even atheists respect him," they eagerly told us.

But when someone said it was strange that a theologically conservative Oxford don married a divorced ex-Communist New Yorker who had moved to England (presumably to escape the McCarthy hearings), all the evangelicals shouted, "He was human." [32] When a few people said there is evidence that he had an affair in his single years after he had become a Christian, a complementarian male said, "He was a man. He who is without sin cast the first stone." When several of us called out Lewis on his racism, sexism, and classism, the complementarians accused us of—you guessed it—political correctness. For their part, the egalitarians said, "Well, he was a man of his times. And he treated Joy Davidman as an equal. Just read *A Grief Observed*." One woman was so sure that if Lewis had lived nowadays, he would have supported women's ordination. Oh, please.

The C. S. Lewis apologists got way too defensive, but I have been in so many discussions where feminists are too diffident about their foremothers' accomplishments. Like C. S. Lewis fans unabashedly praising their golden boy, we should always stand our ground on second wavers' intellectual brilliance, organizational skills, political acumen, and above all, their breathtaking *chutzpah*.

Second-wave feminists deserve as much respect as civil rights activists. Rachel Shteir's summary of *The Feminine Mystique* as "a magnificent if flawed volume whose sum is greater than its parts"[33] applies to practically every second-wave achievement. Don't let anyone trash or trivialize it.

Insist that Female Executives Honor Their Suffragist and Feminist Foremothers

Sheryl Sandberg's 2013 *Lean In: Women, Work, and the Will to Lead* was a sensation. Some said it made feminism cool again. But it didn't take long for Sandberg's global bestseller to get all sorts of criticism, both deserved and harsh, from every corner of the media. One crucial area where the critics were silent was her approach to suffragists and historic feminists. They said nothing and gave her a pass. Quite different from when *Roe v. Wade* was overturned. When Sandberg expressed her shock, activists demanded, "When are you going to make a contribution to Planned Parenthood?" Soon after, she donated one million dollars to that organization. In 2022, she donated three million dollars to abortion rights groups within the American Civil Liberties Union.

When I read *Lean In*, I was amazed by these statements:

> Social gains are never handed out. They must be seized. Leaders of the women's movement—from Susan B. Anthony to Jane Addams to Alice Paul to Bella Abzug to Flo Kennedy to so many others—spoke out loudly and bravely to demand the rights that we now have. Their courage changed our culture and our laws to the benefit of us all. Looking back, it made no sense for my college friends and me to distance ourselves from the hard-won achievements of earlier feminists. We

should have cheered their efforts. Instead, we lowered our voices, thinking the battle was over, and with this reticence we hurt ourselves. [34]

Wow! Did Sheryl Sandberg really say that??? Sheryl Sandberg, the philanthropist and ex-Facebook and Meta executive who used to give the impression that everything would be peachy dandy if women would just *Lean In*????

Yes, she did. It blows my mind. She also made surprisingly good comments about unconscious biases. But because people trivialize women's history, nobody quoted her statements. Nobody *challenged* her to donate to a campaign for suffrage memorials in her current home state during the Nineteenth Amendment Centennial. Women winning the vote in California through a 1911 referendum was a momentous breakthrough for the national movement, and it should never be forgotten.

Philanthropist Melinda French Gates has received considerable media attention for her commitment to protecting and advancing women's rights around the world, especially after her divorce from both Bill Gates and the Gates Foundation. In a recent *Vanity Fair* article, she wisely noted, "Philanthropists are generally more helpful to the world when we're standing behind a movement rather than trying to lead our own." [35]

However, the author never asked French Gates how she was going to honor suffragists and second-wave feminists in Washington state or her native Texas.

Keziah Weir couldn't resist jabbing at nineteenth century women philanthropists:

Emily Bissell, a leading philanthropist over a century ago, was a staunch anti-suffragist because she believed government was men's work, while women's power was best wielded without political entanglements—but

also because she worried that Black women gaining
the vote would loosen the stranglehold wealthy white
women held on that power. [36]

Unfortunately, most female philanthropists of the past were anti-feminist or apolitical, but some were quite the opposite. Keziah Weir should have also mentioned Alva Belmont, who supported the striking shirtwaist workers after the Triangle Shirtwaist Factory Fire in 1911 and was a major financier of the National Woman's Party. Like Melinda French Gates, Alva Belmont also went through a highly publicized divorce. It would have been interesting to hear French Gates's thoughts on Belmont and other feminist philanthropists of the past, including Katharine Dexter McCormick, who financed development of The Pill.

As I write these comments, I can just hear people saying, "Why in the hell are you suggesting that philanthropists finance suffrage memorials? It's 2025. If a company or foundation underwrites a women's suffrage statue nowadays, an anti-DEI group is going to sue it for discrimination against men." I have no illusions about the water we swim in, but to quote Dorothy Height again, "We need to ripen the times." True, most corporations are canceling DEI and they're making sure the world knows it. But a few are defiantly holding onto it while others are trying to build an inclusive workforce in a subtle "mend it, don't end it" way.

As someone who has worked in corporate America for four decades, I have heard executives and management experts constantly talk about the need to recognize high achievers because it builds morale and keeps them from taking their skills to other employers. This commonsense mindset dovetails completely with my view that if women constantly see great activists of the past getting trashed, and if they keep seeing it generation after generation after generation, they're not going to be motivated to "lean in" and continue the work. I doubt that the Melinda French Gateses and Sheryl Sandbergs of the world would have a hard time understanding that basic fact.

As I write this section, I also hear the "But we don't have the money" excuse blaring in the background. Again, the poverty mentality. Pardon the cliché, but we need to think outside the box. Perhaps a Melinda French Gates can't finance statues at this time because of other crucial priorities, but less expensive murals in downtown Seattle and Austin would probably work very well. Melinda French Gates has already donated to the Smithsonian American Women's History Museum in DC, but it hasn't been built yet. Most people are not able to visit the nation's capital, and the Trump administration could kill the project. [37] All history is local, and people need to see that the Nineteenth Amendment and other feminist accomplishments would have never made it without great local activists.

Women's history advocates have told me many depressing stories about proposals that went nowhere with corporations and foundations. However, nobody has ever held their feet to the fire. Nobody has ever accused them of sexism or misogyny if they ignore suffragists and historic feminists. Journalists need to give a detailed suffrage memorial report card on Women's Equality Day and challenge pro-diversity corporations and moderate and progressive philanthropists to step up to the plate.

According to a March 2024 *Fortune* article, women are leading 10 percent of Fortune 500 companies. [38] Yes, it's far from 50 percent, but in 1995, there were no women CEOs in the Fortune 500. People are joking that for the first time in history, women CEOs are outnumbering CEOs named John. [39] Arguably, these women have benefitted from feminism more than anyone else. It's time for all of us—journalists, women's history advocates, those who attend their seminars—to challenge women CEOs, and males as well, to pay their respects by underwriting a suffragist memorial. Don't just ask. Challenge.

In *Half the Sky*, Sheryl WuDunn and Nicholas Kristof stated point-blank that "in recent decades, wealthy American women haven't been particularly generous towards international women's causes." [40] I doubt that their editors urged them to tone down that statement and be nice.

We women's history advocates need to be as frank as WuDunn and Kristof about the stinginess of pro-diversity corporations and progressive foundations towards suffrage memorials. When the world pushes back, we need to lean in and push forward. We may not get everything we want, but at least we will have completely done our part and thrown the ball where it belongs—right smack in the corporate court.

Ensure that Women's Suffrage Events are Powerful

A friend couldn't believe it when I told her that I haven't attended a Women's Equality Day event since 2019. It was partly because of the pandemic, but mainly, it was because I couldn't tolerate the patronizing attitudes anymore. I had voiced my concerns to event organizers, but they had fallen on deaf ears. My friend was shocked, but my decision made sense to her after I mentioned I was writing this book. "Someone who respects suffragists as much as you is not going to put up with put-downs," she said.

Yep. These fantastic activists do not deserve pats on the head followed by academic speeches and condescending reminders to vote and get more women into politics. I would hope that people who attend suffrage events do not need reminders to get off the sofa, trudge over to the polls, and promote feminist women political leaders.

When I drove back to Dallas after a National Votes for Women Trail marker dedication at Wooldridge Square in Austin in late October 2022, I was fuming about the lack of respect for the suffragists we were supposed to honor. There were eight speakers at the event, including Austin City Council Member Kathie Tovo, state Rep. Gina Hinojosa and Democratic Congressman Lloyd Doggett. As shown in Figure 19, the marker noted the rallies at Wooldridge Square and the local leadership of Jane Yelvington McCallum, but we heard very little about her. One speaker said that she passes by McCallum's two-story, light blue house on West 32nd Street every day, but she never mentioned

Photo by Joanne Callahan

Figure 19: National Votes for Women Trail marker for Jane Yelvington McCallum at Wooldridge Square in Austin.

how McCallum and her supportive husband, Arthur, as parents of five children, remain relevant to twenty-first century two-career couples.

As part of a pioneering power couple, Jane led suffrage organizations, wrote newspaper columns, was one of the first mothers to attend the University of Texas at Austin (UT Austin), lobbied the Texas Congress for progressive reforms, was secretary of state from 1927 to 1933, and advocated for women to get on juries. Arthur was superintendent of Austin Public Schools. When the school board told Arthur to keep Jane out of politics, he replied that they could threaten to fire him but not his wife. [41] In an age of trad wives and zoomer men who think "patriarchy works better for everyone," we need to tell stories about people like Jane and Arthur, and we need to tell them to young couples. And yes, their kids turned out fine.

In his speech, Lloyd Doggett rightly emphasized current voter suppression issues, threats to democracy, and the curtailment of women's reproductive rights. He also acknowledged the 2017 Women's March in Austin, in which I and several other audience members participated. But his speech would have been much more powerful if he had quoted Jane Yelvington McCallum: "Somehow I felt too thankful to be jubilant. We have a great responsibility, and I pray God we may meet it squarely and successfully."[42]

After the Austin event, I started to think about how we could make women's suffrage events more powerful and have come up with these suggestions:

• **Start with a moment of silence.** Even if the event is not about the suffragists who went to prison, we still need to honor them. Alice Paul and others could have been killed for fighting for our rights. The moment of silence should also honor suffragists who made other types of sacrifices: Inez Milholland's martyrdom; Black, Hispanic, Native and Asian American suffragists who had to fight both racism and sexism; and suffragists whose husbands abused them.

At the Austin event, Catherine Alvarado Cilfone, who represented the National Collaborative for Women's History Sites, was one of the last speakers. She was the only person who called the suffragists great Americans. She also mentioned Clara Snell Wolfe's local NWP leadership.

Again, there should have been a moment of silence at the beginning of the Austin event. A speaker should have lauded the heroism of Elizabeth Kalb, Lucille Shields, Maud Sampson Williams, Jovita Idar, and the sacrifices of all other Texas suffragists. The moment of silence should have been followed by music, poetry, or a short dramatization.

• **Tell the world what made that suffragist great.** This is the time to unabashedly toot her horn, to honor her and not just acknowledge her. As someone who has never seen a suffragist get idolized, I am not concerned about speakers indulging in hagiography. At least, not yet. I'm worried about them being too modest.

Jane Yelvington McCallum led such a rich life that it is a shame that none of the speakers talked about this great Texan. *They should have emphasized that she acted like a voter before she won the vote.* In 1917, she and other concerned Austinites organized a public demonstration against Gov. James Ferguson mainly because of his "my way or the highway" attitude towards UT Austin. Because the university refused to fire faculty members he found objectionable, he vetoed the appropriations for the school. In McCallum's speech, she called him an "implacable foe of woman suffrage and of every great moral issue for which women stood." [43] That rally helped turn public opinion against Ferguson and helped pave the way for his impeachment.

• **Use the event as a springboard for suffrage history activism.** I have never been to a suffrage event that passed a petition to make Women's Equality Day a federal holiday or that ended with a protest march at a local history or art museum about its neglect of the great suffragists. No wonder so many suffrage events are so bland.

I am not suggesting that we use these events as springboards for activism just to make them more interesting. I am making this suggestion so that these great Americans will never be forgotten or trivialized, and so that someday, we will not need to educate the world about the achievements of Alice Paul, Maud Sampson Williams, Carrie Chapman Catt, Jovita Idar, Minnie Fisher Cunningham, and so many other superb trailblazers. I would bet that most people forget about suffragists the day after a suffrage event.

During the Austin event, Council Member Kathie Tovo said that her daughter couldn't imagine a time when women couldn't vote and gave that "How can I make her see the light?" look. I was disappointed that she didn't elaborate. If I were in her shoes, how would I have handled that moment with an impressionable young daughter? And how would I have translated it to reach the audience at this important event, which ought to have so much potential? I hope I would have taken the opportunity to put ideas in motion. I would have said:

> Like most parents, I am frustrated. I would like to see
> a great TV series about the suffrage movement, a series

as gripping as *A French Village*. It gave me such a vivid picture of what it was like to live in France during the Nazi occupation and made me realize why people acted the way they did. I think if my daughter saw an exceptional TV series, she would understand and would be less likely to fall into the trap of political apathy.

I know it's going to take decades to get that series, but in the meantime, I have made an appointment with the director of the Bullock Texas State History Museum to work on ways that it can better publicize the suffragists' accomplishments. We're going to meet on November 12 at 2 p.m., and you're welcome to join me. Just email an RSVP to me by November 9, COB.

State Rep. Gina Hinojosa, one of the few speakers who actually talked about the suffragists, didn't say anything about Jane Yelvington McCallum, but she did mention Minnie Fisher Cunningham, who gave several speeches during the Wooldridge Square rallies. I liked her tribute: "Minnie Fisher Cunningham's 'we'll vote for you if you vote for us' tactic may seem cynical, but that is the way things get done in politics." Yes, Minniefish was as politically sophisticated as they come. After the event, I briefly talked to Hinojosa about the need for a suffrage statue on the humongous lawn at the state Capitol. She seemed excited about it. She gave me her card and said, "Let's talk about it."

But I didn't take her up on it. I had the usual excuses: she probably won't respond; she was just being nice when she showed enthusiasm; she's dealing with a lot of right-wing extremists in the legislature and doesn't have time; I don't have the money and connections to turn my idea into reality; I'm so tired. In retrospect, I should have "leaned in" and called her. Even if nothing came out of it, I could rest assured that I had done my part.

- **End with an exhortation to keep fighting the good fight and**

ensuring that the suffragists' sacrifices are never forgotten. As I said before, most suffrage events urge us to vote and help more women get into public office. But the suffs didn't want us to vote just for voting's sake. They wanted us to vote women into office so that we would build a better world and a much less oppressive society for all women.

The speakers need to encourage people to vote for pro-democracy candidates who will fight for global human rights. Support women politicians who do feminist activism. Yes, there will probably be anti-feminists in the audience, but the fact is that conservative women in Congress would have never made it without suffragist and feminist activism.

Speakers also need to exhort us to fight for the suffragists. Otherwise, it will look like we are just using them in the same way that people who don't like their mothers will grudgingly admit, "But she did make a lot of sacrifices for me. I would have never gotten an engineering degree and a good job if she hadn't made me do my homework."

I know someone is going to demand, "How will we talk about the suffragists' flaws?" In the "Why Many Say White Suffragists Were Racists" section of this book, I talked at length about how, during the Austin event, Kathie Tovo and Gloria Mata Pennington lectured the audience about Black suffragists and segregation in the movement. I also talked about how I have never heard any lecturing at military and civil rights events.

For starters, stop the double standard. If we're going to lecture the audience about racism in the suffrage movement, we need to do the same at events honoring civil rights activists. Give people a lecture about the activists' misogyny. However, when I attend an event that is supposed to honor someone, a lecture about his or her flaws is a turnoff.

Nevertheless, I don't want any hagiography. To ward off idolatry, I suggest that at the beginning of the event, a speaker tell us that, say, Jane Yelvington McCallum was in some ways a woman of her time. Like all of us, she had her flaws and had to play realpolitik, which you can learn about in numerous books, articles, and social media posts.

But she was a tremendous women's suffrage activist and that is why we are honoring her.

It certainly wouldn't bother me if speakers talked about the fact that we're far from political, economic, and social equality and urged the audience to agitate for equal rights laws. But we already have Domestic Violence Awareness Month, International Women's Day, and Equal Pay Days for Black, Hispanic, Native American, and Asian American Pacific Islander women. The mass media still pays attention to these bread-and-butter issues. Many journalists use Mother's Day and Father's Day as a springboard to raise consciousness on discrimination against breadwinner mothers and men's uphill battles to be good fathers in this society. Since suffragists are always in danger of getting dumped into the historical ash heap, it's only fair that suffragist events keep the spotlight on the suffs. Without their stunning accomplishments, we would have never been able to advocate for other feminist issues and American women's reality would be much grimmer than it is in 2025.

Show History Teachers How to Educate Students About the Women's Suffrage Movement

I feel uneasy about writing this section, because I know that many teachers are burned out and are thinking of leaving the profession. Weaponized controversies over critical race theory, banned books, and DEI are hardly the ideal backdrops for motivating history and social studies teachers to start educating students about women's suffrage.

And yet, I wouldn't be doing justice to the suffs if I ignored the history class issue. In the twenty-first century, teachers at all levels, from kindergarten to graduate school, have a wealth of tools to help them plan lessons that avoid the "sit still, listen to a lecture, and take notes" style of learning. We now have books, documentaries, plays, and movies that make suffrage history come alive. *A Mighty Girl* is a great online clearinghouse of books designed for children of all ages. I enjoyed Natalie Proulx's NYT essay, "19 Ways to Teach the Nineteenth Amendment," with its emphasis on interactive lessons. [44]

But these resources assume that students want to learn; that principals are supportive; that parents are delighted that their children will learn about a movement that was barely mentioned twenty years ago. And there is an assumption that the Trump administration will be thrilled to issue a presidential proclamation on Women's Equality Day even though it has canceled proclamations on all other identity-based events. Above all, they assume that teachers will magically be able to coordinate women's suffrage lessons with other necessary lessons. Those lessons include the First Americans; the Viking, Spanish, Puritan, and Jamestown settlements; the Revolutionary War; the Industrial Revolution; the Westward Expansion; the Trail of Tears; the Abolitionist Movement; the Temperance Movement; the Civil War and Reconstruction; the Gilded Age; WWI; the Great Depression; WWII; the Cold War; the Korean War; the Vietnam War; the Civil Rights Movement; the Feminist Movement; 9-11; and so on.

Adding the Women's Suffrage Movement to history lessons seems overwhelming, but help is on the way. Kelsie Brook Eckert, executive director of the Remedial Herstory Project and Coordinator of Social Studies Education at Plymouth State University, is providing tools to help history and social studies teachers weave women's history into their classes. When I first saw her book, *Teaching Women's History: Breaking Barriers and Undoing Male Centrism in K-12 Social Studies*, I thought it would be a dry academic treatise. But it was surprisingly practical and deeply personal.

Eckert won the New Hampshire History Teacher of the Year award twice and has paid her dues in the trenches. When she taught in rural schools, she learned very quickly that students would not let her say, "feminist." As a married mother of two sons, she knows we live in the age of Jordan Peterson, Andrew Tate, and Moms for Liberty. She has been criticized a great deal—most frequently from those on the right:

No one ever criticized my use of *A Patriot's History of the United States*, whose introduction includes an explicitly conservative intention . . . Not once did anyone ever complain that I had students read excerpts from Adolf Hitler's book, *Mein Kampf.* Not one criticism. What does this tell me?[45]

She has no problem admitting that textbooks, state standards, and teacher education programs are sexist barriers and that they violate the letter and spirit of Title IX. To top it off, social studies and history classes have been devalued.[46] But she urges teachers to face their fears and take the courageous step of teaching a more inclusive history.

To anyone who complains about not having time to integrate women into history classes, Eckert says, "Teachers toss and reprioritize the curriculum as it becomes culturally relevant and timely."[47] History textbooks get updated with each cultural milestone and presidential administration. Teachers still had time to teach about the Revolutionary War after textbooks started covering 9/11 and the War on Terror. Eckert's book showed me that good history teachers make the time to teach students about the Women's Suffrage Movement. Her stories reminded me of an acquaintance who complained about her high school history teacher, a coach, wasting a lot of time talking about Davy Crockett. Even conservative boys in the class started rolling their eyes.

Eckert makes a strong case against the pop-up method of teaching women's history, whereby the Women's Suffrage Movement is separated from other topics. She lists several types of historical periodization that make it easier to include women. One of the most basic is:
- Early America: 1600-1820
- America's Many Frontiers: 1820-1880
- Modern America: 1880-1920
- Stormy America: 1920-1945
- A Global Transformation: 1945-present
- Twenty-First Century, an Old Battle Reformed and Begun Anew[48]

In each of these periods, teachers would talk about the lives of women of all races, religions, and classes, with information about their rights (or lack thereof). The Women's Suffrage Movement would be integrated with the rest of history, and it wouldn't feel like an add-on feature.

Obviously, teachers need to develop expertise in women's history before they can integrate it into their classes. But they're not going to learn it from a textbook. Eckert recommends that they take Women's Studies (WS) courses and learn about pedagogies that encourage gender equality. However, I have found that WS is a mixed bag, just like everything else. There are no nationally approved standards, so students may go through a beginning WS class without delving much into the Women's Suffrage Movement.

If they can't find a WS class that covers women's suffrage in any detail, they will need to educate themselves and consult with those who are teaching their students about the Women's Suffrage Movement. And they need to be on the lookout for biases against the suffs. As I have shown throughout this book, suffragists can get denigrated even when they get memorials. A person could teach an "inclusive" history and still be misogynistic and racist.

Eckert puts a lot of responsibility on individual teachers, but progressive students and parents need to support them. They need the same attitude as the students in *La Historia Oficial*, a riveting Argentine film about the impact of the Dirty War on an affluent high school history teacher. When she teaches "the official story" about the government atrocities at an exclusive boys' prep school, some of her students and a progressive teacher challenge her. "History textbooks are written by murderers," one says. The film focuses on her painful discovery of the truth and how it completely changes her life.

In 2017, I got together with several friends for a discussion with my then-congressman, Pete Sessions. I asked him if the budget was going to impact the funding for the Belmont-Paul Women's Equality National Monument and other women's history memorials. I then talked about Alice Paul and Alva Belmont. He blithely said he had never heard of

Alice Paul. I shot back, "You have a degree in American history, and you never heard of Alice Paul???" He got defensive and told me that he knows a lot about the Women's Suffrage Movement. I laughed and briefly rolled my eyes.

A historian told me I was somewhat unfair to Pete Sessions because history teachers never talked about Alice Paul during Sessions's college days. I strongly disagreed. I never learned about Alice Paul in my history classes, and I have never taken a Women's Studies class. Yet I educated myself, and it wasn't difficult. Most history teachers are not going to cover the Women's Suffrage Movement until parents, students, and tax-paying constituents expect it. And that means we need to take the risk of challenging them while acknowledging the pressures they face.

Fortunately, we can now tell them about Kelsie Brook Eckert's book and Remedial Herstory Project website. And we can show them a treasure trove of wonderful stories. To quote Anne Varner,

> When we remember these women, we can become inspired, empowered, and enlightened. History helps us to learn about ourselves and reminds us to continue to strive for greatness. [49]

Rebrand Women's Equality Day and Call It Nineteenth Amendment Day

In 2023, Barbara Hood, a retired attorney living in Alaska, wrote an opinion piece, "Reclaiming Women's Equality Day." She was not happy about the fact that National Dog Day is also on August 26 and that it is much more popular than Women's Equality Day. Hood emphasized that she loves pooches and had a golden retriever who lived for sixteen years and is buried in her yard. However, Women's Equality Day is sacred, and she will celebrate dogs on August 27. As Hood elaborates:

Today women enjoy rights and privileges that our mothers and grandmothers hardly could have imagined. The past teaches us that these advancements didn't just materialize but were gained through the vision and tenacity of generations before us. The past also teaches us that complacency about our rights and privileges lays the groundwork for their erosion. In these times when women's rights remain under attack both at home and abroad, **it's more important than ever to understand what women stand to lose if we forget our history.** [50]

Women's Equality Day has been a failure. In a culture that denigrates and "matricides" suffragists even when it builds monuments to them, it's hardly a shock that so few people commemorate it, even in feminist groups. The people who pay homage usually give suffragists nothing more than a patronizing pat on the head.

And yet, in honor of the intellectual brilliance, the stunning innovations, the tremendous political acumen, and heroism of the suffragists, we must reclaim and rebrand Women's Equality Day (WED). To ignore WED and let National Dog Day take over is a profound insult. It tells the world that America thinks women's rights are trivial.

We have federal holidays for Martin Luther King, for presidents, for those who died in wars, for Juneteenth, for the Declaration of Independence, for workers, and for veterans. But nothing for those who valiantly fought for women to have a voice in the American political system, to be "citizens at last" so that we could build a post-patriarchal society where the talents of women of all races, religions, ethnic groups, classes, and sexualities are honored as much as the talents of men. Again, it shows the world the misogynistic underbelly of American culture.

When Bella Abzug introduced Women's Equality Day legislation in 1971, the women's movement was on a roll. Activists had celebrated stunning victories with the Women's Strike for Equality marches held on August 26, 1970. The Supreme Court was starting to use the Fourteen Amendment's equal protection clause in sex discrimination cases. The Equal Rights Amendment was on the verge of a breakthrough in Congress. The editors and staff at *Ms.* magazine were preparing to publish the first issue, which sold out eight days after it was released. No wonder Abzug called August 26 Women's Equality Day.

But who wants to commemorate Women's Equality Day in a world where Hillary Rodham Clinton and Kamala Harris lost to Trump; where most husbands do not take equal responsibility for housework, childcare, and emotional labor; where Pornhub is one of the world's most visited websites; where violence against women, sexual harassment, the glass ceiling, and the sticky floor are still facts of life; and where suffragists and historic feminists are denigrated? For most of us, it's Women's INEQUALITY Day.

Yes, the phrase, Women's Equality Day, is aspirational, but in twenty-first century America, it has become a depressant. The time has come to change the name to Nineteenth Amendment Day. A few friends don't like the new name because it doesn't contain the word "woman," but it still has several advantages:

> • Concentrating on the amendment avoids the fantasy that women already have equality.

> • It focuses on the greatest single expansion of voters in the republic, one of the most breathtaking victories in the history of the United States.

> • It acknowledges the limitations of this great victory: Jim Crow laws, Asian immigrants forbidden from becoming citizens, husbands who kept their wives from going to the polls, and so on.

• It focuses on a victory that enabled women to start fighting for equal rights, a victory that led Crystal Eastman to declare, "Now we can begin."

• It tells the world that most Americans have some respect for women's rights.

• It inspires us to take cues from these brilliant, heroic women and their male allies and keep marching as we battle the backlashes in the age of Trump.

Ten years ago, I would have had a problem with saying Nineteenth Amendment Day because so few people knew about "the women's suffrage law." But in an age of *The 19th* News*, I have no worries. When I mention the Nineteenth Amendment nowadays, very few people give me a deer-in-the-headlights look.

Getting the name change on the books will take a tremendous amount of time and activism, as shown by the zigzag history of Indigenous Peoples Day. During the Reagan administration, activists held alternative Indigenous Peoples Day commemorations on Columbus Day. After several decades of activism, the idea got traction. Amazingly, the Dallas City Council recognized Indigenous Peoples Day in 2019. Although not a federal holiday, the Biden administration formally recognized it in 2021.

The name change has generated significant controversy in the Italian-American community. New York and Boston, with their tremendous Italian immigrant legacies, have worked on ways to honor both indigenous peoples and Americans of Italian descent on the same day. But that tension pales next to the vitriol of the Trump administration. Trump has not issued an executive order to recognize Indigenous Peoples Day. Trump has a traditional view of Columbus Day and rails against a "woke" approach to history. But many will still pay their respects to the first Americans on Columbus Day, just like in the Reagan days.

The obvious takeaway for Nineteenth Amendment Day activists is to be patient, persistent, and flexible. We obviously need to sell women's history organizations on the name change and get local governments and, someday, a progressive president to recognize it. But I have already started to say "Nineteenth Amendment Day, also known as Women's Equality Day" in my speeches on the Women's Suffrage Movement and to explain my position.

Nevertheless, the issue with Women's "Equality" Day is deeper than the problematic name. It's primarily about honor and how we should show it.

Do Women's History Activism on Nineteenth Amendment Day and during Women's History Month

I have read Women's Equality Day proclamations from every president who issued them, from Nixon in 1973 all the way to Biden in 2024. They follow the usual template: an acknowledgment of the suffragists' courage, persistence, and determination; an admission that there is still discrimination against women; and a summary of what their administration has done for women. Some sounded more like campaign speeches than a moment to honor great Americans.

A few proclamations mentioned real flesh-and-blood activists: Abigail Adams, Elizabeth Cady Stanton, Sojourner Truth, Alice Paul, Carrie Chapman Catt, Ida B. Wells, and others. Indeed, Trump made sure the whole world knew that he had pardoned Susan B. Anthony for illegally voting, which prompted Deborah Hughes, CEO of the Susan B. Anthony Museum, to retort, "Objection! Mr. President, Susan B. Anthony must decline your offer of a pardon." [51]

In their proclamations, Nixon, Ford, and several Democratic presidents reiterated their support for the ERA. Biden noted that the voting rights of non-white women did not get enforced until the Voting Rights Act of 1965.

But so much was missing from every single one of those proclamations. They did not honor the suffragists' intellectual brilliance, activist innovations, political sophistication, and heroism. They were silent about how suffragists get shortchanged in history textbooks. They never criticized those who created other holidays on Women's Equality Day. (We're looking at you, National Dog Day.)

I was shocked that no president ever mentioned any achievements on suffrage history preservation. Obama never mentioned his designation of the Belmont-Paul Women's Equality National Monument. Predictably, no president ever said that Women's Equality Day should become a federal holiday.

I know that much has changed since 2024. Trump will probably direct all agencies to ignore Women's Equality Day. But we still need to ripen the time and push future presidents to issue better proclamations.

We certainly need more eloquent suffrage events. In almost every section of this chapter, I have given ideas on how to honor suffragists. Those ideas would certainly work on Nineteenth Amendment Day, and I already have more:

• Have a postcard party where people write to the Central Park Conservancy and urge the leaders to fix the insulting description next to the Women's Rights Pioneers Monument. This postcard party could take place at several restaurants throughout Manhattan, at a suffrage cocktail party at the Hermitage Hotel in Nashville, at a backyard pool party in Dallas, and a beach party in San Diego.

• Commission Kelsie Brook Eckert to lead a short training session on teaching middle and high school students the basics about the Women's Suffrage Movement, and how to deal with flak from administrators, parents, and students, especially in the age of Trump.

• This one is high risk, but I'll mention it anyway. If you are a college student, report on what your history professor said—and didn't say—about the Women's Suffrage Movement. Compare notes with other students' history professors and publicize them either in the school newspaper or on a website or blog. Report your findings during a Nineteenth Amendment Day party, or even to the media.

The list of ideas is endless. We just need to use political will.

As for Women's History Month, it's just a patronizing pat on the head. I have never heard of any activism in March or any other month to get publishers to integrate women's great, underrated, and often forgotten accomplishments into history textbooks or to expose the double standards in bestselling or critically acclaimed history books and films.

Many women have privately agreed with me that presidential proclamations on Women's History Month have been condescending and that celebrations at corporations have usually been insulting. And yet, most feminists and women's history advocates have remained silent. To quote historian Nancy Goldstone:

> . . . we have allowed ourselves to be contented with the sop of parallel studies and a single month devoted to women's achievements. It takes the heat off conservative academics who think that female influence is overrated . . . [52]

But what if the National Women's History Alliance (NWHA), Veteran Feminists of America (VFA) and other women's history groups had led a series of protest email campaigns to those conservative academics and provided strong evidence that women's achievements are not overrated? What if NWHA and VFA had posted the protest e-mails on their websites? What if we had sent massive protest letters to the media during Women's History Month?

Goldstone thinks Women's History Month is a mistake. I understand her frustration, but women's history will not get integrated into the curriculum without a persistent movement. Women's History Month, if continuously done with a strong feminist activist spirit, could galvanize that movement.

Each year, NWHA has a theme for Women's History Month. I

was not inspired by NWHA themes like "Celebrating Women Who Tell Our Stories" (2023) or "Women Providing Healing, Promoting Hope" (2022). However, I would have paid more attention if NWHA had led a campaign to ensure that the women scientists who co-led the development of the COVID vaccine (Kizzmekia Corbett, Özlem Türeci, Kathrin Jansen, Nobel Prize winner Katalin Karikó, and others) get the recognition they deserve in science history books. History has shown again and again that there is no guarantee that they will be remembered.

"Well-behaved women seldom make history," historian Laurel Thatcher Ulrich loves to say. This is an opportunity for us to behave very badly. We can commemorate the holiday on our own, stop the pats on the head to great women, and sow winter wheat for it to become a powerful impetus to make history books and films treat them with the respect they deserve.

Sow Winter Wheat for a Movement to Make Nineteenth Amendment Day a Federal Holiday

I started this chapter with Dorothy Height's advice to ripen the time if the time isn't ripe, a statement that reminds me of a political climate akin to a moderate winter, where we have a few "Snowmageddons" and several blistery cold days but also many nice days that look forward to spring. Ripening the time works well for tasks that individuals can perform to move us closer to attaining true respect for the suffragists.

"We are sowing winter wheat for future generations," Elizabeth Cady Stanton once said. That quote springs to mind when I think of the movement to make Nineteenth Amendment Day a federal holiday. The political climate is freezing, with very few nice days that point to spring. And yet, winter wheat, if nurtured correctly, produces delicious bread during the time of harvest.

It will be a huge uphill struggle to convince Congress to authorize a federal holiday, which is why I find Opal Lee's "winter wheat" journey so inspiring. She started her Juneteenth activism in the 1970s. Her breakthrough came when she and other Juneteenth activists seized the moment during the George Floyd Black Lives Matter protests. In a near miracle, Congress put the holiday on the books. Juneteenth is vulnerable in the age of Trump, but many of us will still commemorate it regardless of what Congress does.

I have talked to women's history advocates about making Nineteenth Amendment Day a federal holiday, but several think that International Women's Day (IWD) would be a better candidate. March 8 is close to the beginning of spring and, in theory, IWD covers the whole spectrum of global women's rights activism.

However, far too many people confuse IWD with Valentine's Day. I've heard liberal reconciling United Methodist pastors call IWD a time to "affirm the women in your life." Male disc jockeys have said IWD is a time to "tell the woman in your life how much you love her." Oh, please. These inane comments make me want to call it International FEMINIST Day.

We all know how a campaign for International Feminist Day would fare in Congress or in the general culture. Even if we stuck with International Women's Day, its socialist roots would be enough to give conservative Republican politicians, both female and male, an excuse to dump it into the ash heap.

A strong selling point for Nineteenth Amendment Day is that it commemorates an American victory. Without that amendment, the Voting Rights Act of 1965 would have been for men only in states that didn't allow women to vote. The Nineteenth Amendment enabled American women of all races, classes, religions, and sexualities to fight for legal birth control, equal pay laws, Title IX, the Violence Against Women Act, ERA, and so on. Enforcement of these laws has always been uneven, but the law is a teaching tool, and the feminist activists behind these laws and their enforcement changed America for the better.

I know August 26 is one of the hottest days of summer. Hey, I was raised in Phoenix, and I currently live in Dallas. But hot weather hasn't stopped Congress from declaring federal holidays on June 19, July 4, and the first Monday of September. A holiday on August 26 is a nice way to ease into Labor Day, just like Juneteenth is a pleasant way to ramp up for the Fourth of July.

To remain passive about making Nineteenth Amendment Day a federal holiday is to say that women's rights are trivial, that suffragists do not deserve top recognition, and that it's OK in the beacon of democracy (albeit a shaky democracy) to treat women as inferiors.

As I reflect on what it will take to make Nineteenth Amendment Day a federal holiday, I think of Opal Lee's Juneteenth journey. Juneteenth was commemorated in African American communities long before Lee came on the scene. When Lee started her Juneteenth activism in the 1970s, she already had a wealth of experience as a teacher and manager of nonprofits. She had a great sense of symbolism and political theater. And yes, she was persistent.

Obviously, we're at ground zero for Nineteenth Amendment Day, especially with the "matriciding" of suffragists. Every time we write a book, do a podcast, commission a statue, and unveil a memorial, we need to present the suffragists in such a way that the audience will think, "We need a federal holiday." We need to make every Nineteenth Amendment Day commemoration a compelling springboard for suffrage history activism, including the push for that day off.

I believe that if we do a good job of laying the groundwork, leaders will emerge and become the public faces of the movement. I already see the possibilities for great political theater. The skydivers who made such a wonderful impression during the Suffrage Centennial could do a show in several areas of the country every year. Mixologists could provide nineteen different suffrage drinks—cocktails, mocktails, coffees, teas, and even craft beers—at the Hermitage in Nashville on Nineteenth Amendment Day.

Lee's 2.5-mile walk each year to represent the 2.5 years it took for news of the Emancipation Proclamation to reach Texas could be adapted to the Nineteenth Amendment Day campaign. Throughout the country on August 26, activists could walk or run 1.9 miles on the beach, take a 1.9-mile hike in cooler areas, and swim or pool jog nineteen yards in the hot spots. In a variation of Lee's symbolic walk from Fort Worth to Washington, DC, in the fall and winter of 2016, we could take a symbolic walk from Seneca Falls to the White House.

Federal holidays are not a panacea. Martin Luther King Day is guilty of idolatry, and it shortchanges other great civil rights activists. Veterans were so disgusted with Memorial Day becoming known as the day that the swimming pool opens that they started the Carry the Load campaign. The Fourth of July is an excuse for a barbecue with fireworks and patriotic music. Labor Day is the end of summer.

Skeptics remind us that Juneteenth has not improved the teaching about slavery and the Civil War in our schools. They also remind us that if Nineteenth Amendment Day became a federal holiday, there would still be a multitude of Americans who know nothing about Alice Paul and Mary Church Terrell and don't want to learn.

And yet, if Congress voted to abolish these holidays, the skeptics would be the first to protest. Federal holidays are tremendous opportunities to pay our respects, improve our political education, reflect on the future, and start doing activism. I learned more about the Revolutionary War and the labor movement through good articles and documentaries on the Fourth of July and Labor Day than I ever did in my history classes. Presidents Day was a springboard for protesting Trump and Musk's threats to democracy in 2025. I participated in the No Kings on Presidents Day rally at the Dallas Convention Center.

We live in a time when anti-suffragists are coming out of the shadows. They have always been around, but most of us thought we could ignore them. And then, House Republicans passed the SAVE Act, a bill that would require citizens to have a passport or birth certificate matching their names before they could vote. The SAVE Act has not passed the Senate as of this writing, but many women suspect that it is a voter suppression tactic against married women since a large majority still take their husbands' names and many don't have passports. Sarah Stankorb and Amanda Marcotte have written extensively about Christian nationalists who hate the Nineteenth Amendment and promote "household voting," whereby the husband, as the "head" of the family, is the person who casts the ballot.[53]

Secular anti-suffragists are also making inroads, but in a more insidious way. Curtis Yarvin, an engineer lauded by several Silicon Valley billionaires, thinks American democracy should be replaced by a monarchy run by a CEO, his euphemism for a dictator. "When I look at the status of women in, say, a Jane Austen novel, which is well before enfranchisement, it actually seems kind of OK," he said in an NYT interview.[54] And what does he think about women's suffrage? "I don't believe in voting at all," he said.[55] Yarvin claims that he doesn't vote.

From Christian nationalists who believe women's suffrage is evil to history teachers who lie about not having the time to cover the movement to the "matriciding" of white suffragists because they weren't twenty-first century intersectional to trad wives thinking household voting sounds so sweet . . . the varieties of misogyny throughout the political spectrum in this country seem infinite. As I have shown so many times, most memorials don't honor the suffragists. And yet, both anti-suffragists and "matriciders" make me want to double down on making Nineteenth Amendment Day a federal holiday.

I know we have plenty of fires to fight in the age of Trump, but we can still lay the groundwork for a halfway-decent women's suffrage holiday. Making Nineteenth Amendment Day a federal holiday would send a powerful message: *This amendment is so sacred that we are honoring the brilliant, heroic suffragists who made it happen. Christian nationalists or any other anti-suffragists who touch it will pay a price.*

Even if Congress never authorizes Nineteenth Amendment Day, it is worth it to aim for that federal holiday because it is motivation for us to stop denigrating suffragists, improve our memorials, and treat them with the respect they deserve.

So please, put on your jacket, get a shovel, get out of the house, and start sowing that winter wheat. Naysayers abound, but they cannot take away one basic fact about suffragists.

These early feminists were GIANTS.

*"How we treat our elders says a lot about
who we are as a society, and we need to do better."*
Chloé Zhao, film director [1]

*"If they don't give you a seat at the table,
bring a folding chair."*
Shirley Chisholm, politician

*"Hands off the suffragists.
Hands off the Nineteenth Amendment."*
Joanne Callahan, women's history activist

Epilogue

In an interview with Gloria Steinem, where the interviewer was obviously playing gotcha games, the legendary activist was asked if she had any regrets about feminism.

Her answer? "Yes, we've been much too nice." [2]

My thoughts exactly, especially about the way we promote the history of the Women's Suffrage Movement. Throughout this book, I have shown how being too nice has hurt the legacy of great suffragists and kept them from getting the honor they deserve.

I want to see women's history advocates stop being so ladylike. I want to see them unabashedly fight for suffragists in the same way historians fight for Abraham Lincoln, John Muir, and Frederick Douglass.

While I was writing this book, I was also protesting the authoritarian disruptions of Trump and Musk. As I was driving home from a Hands Off rally, I reflected on the upcoming America250 commemoration and realized that "hands off" can also apply to attacks and put-downs of suffragists and historic feminists. "Hands off" means leave it alone. It can also mean don't trivialize, degrade, exploit, patronize, or cancel.

When a progressive congressman says he promotes statues of suffragists because they're good role models for his daughters, we need to tell him, "Hands off. *You also need to promote them because they're excellent role models for you and your sons.*"

When suffragists and historic feminists get trivialized in America250 presentations, or when historians imply that women's history exists just to make women feel good about themselves, we need to shout out, "Hands off. Women's history is not a self-esteem course for young girls. It exists because mainstream history is inaccurate, and it discriminates against women."

Above all, if Carrie Chapman Catt is absent from the proposed suffrage statue on the Capitol Mall, we need to proclaim from the rooftops, "Hands off. Snubbing a great suffragist who did over thirty years of powerful activism and played a leading role in ratifying the Nineteenth Amendment is an act of matricide."

Shortly after Trump started his tariff war and declared it a day of "liberation," Katha Pollitt asked in her column in the *Nation*, "How Far Will Eight Years of Trump Set Back American Women?" Pollitt admits that for years, she resisted the view that feminism was in retreat. She thought that women's liberation was unstoppable, even though progress was often slow and there were devastating setbacks. But Trump, J. D. Vance, Musk, Pete Hegseth, Robert F. Kennedy Junior, and that "monstrous regiment of misogynists" around the world have forced her to come to grips with the fact that the administration is determined to

Make America Guyland Again. Pollitt gives a devastating summary of all the cuts to programs that benefit women:

> Equality, gender, and women are now on a government blacklist of some two hundred fifty words that will get your grants canceled and your scientific research defunded—along with racism, Black, LGBT, and disabled. (Men is OK.)[3]

As much as I liked Pollitt's article, I have never believed that women's liberation was unstoppable. How could I when I was so acutely aware of the "matriciding" of suffragists and historical feminists? Because activists generally didn't get the recognition they deserved and backlash usually came after a breakthrough, progress sometimes felt slippery, especially when I contrasted it with the lionization of the founding fathers, male civil rights activists, and male World War II veterans.

This "matricide" made me reluctant to do women's rights activism, but I did it anyway because the misogyny was so wrong and painful, and the suffragists' "We may be defeated but we will NOT surrender" spirit was so irresistible.

That wonderfully badass, no-surrender activism will be on full display in the *Suffs* cross-country tour that started in September 2025. There are big plans for parties at the Hermitage when *Suffs* comes to Nashville in March 2026, and I'm excited about *Suffs* coming to Bass Performance Hall in Fort Worth in August 2026. It is a wonderful opportunity to take Shirley Chisholm's advice to bring a folding chair if you don't get a seat at the table.

Even if *Suffs* doesn't call out the discrimination against suffragists and other great women in our history textbooks and the cast and crew don't tell the world that Nineteenth Amendment Day must become a federal holiday, speak out during the show. Bring a picket sign, mention these issues during the talkback session, and share articles about these items with others during intermission. Sow winter wheat, ripen the times, and make *Suffs* a springboard for long-term women's history activism.

Laila Erica Drew, the actor who played both Phyllis Terrell and Robin, a NOW activist, in the Broadway production of *Suffs*, provides a great example. After a demonstration that attacked the "white feminism" of *Suffs*, Drew posted a response on Instagram:

> Since we wanna (sic) talk about erasure, thanks for trying to erase the work I do in this show. Now I definitely know nobody cares that I'm baring my soul and my ancestral pain on stage every single night, especially the people who claim to be fighting for us but in the same breath say they want to "cancel" one of the only shows on Broadway that addresses Black erasure. It seems we have forgotten who the real enemy is in this fight. You wanna protest? You wanna make a difference? Do something for the people you claim to fight for. [4]

As I write these words, I have also read Amanda Marcotte's article about "family values" Speaker of the House Mike Johnson trying to block a bill that would let House members on parental leave vote by proxy, aided by technology. [5] He didn't succeed, but Project 2025 is not giving up. What will they think of next?

Regardless of any new voter suppression stunts that the MAGA crowd pulls during the *Suffs* tour, or any new attacks from progressives on the Women's Suffrage Movement, we all need to say with complete conviction . . .

Hands off the suffragists!
Hands off the Nineteenth Amendment!
Hands off the Fifteenth Amendment and the Voting Rights Act!
STOP THE MATRICIDE!

ENDNOTES

INTRODUCTION

1. "Isabel Allende > Quotes," Goodreads, https://www.goodreads.com/author/quotes/2238.Isabel_Allende

2. Mary Louise Roberts, *What Soldiers Do: Sex and the American GI in World War II France* (Chicago: University of Chicago Press, 2013).

3. Customer reviews, Mary Louise Roberts's *What Soldiers Do: Sex and the American GI in World War II France*, Amazon, https://www.amazon.com/What-Soldiers-Do-American-France/product-reviews/0226923096/ref=cm_cr_getr_d_paging_btm_prev_1?ie=UTF8&reviewerType=all_reviews&pageNumber=1.

4. Christiane Amanpour, "Remembering D-Day 80 Years Later," *Apple Podcast*, June 6, 2024, https://podcasts.apple.com/ca/podcast/remembering-d-day-80-years-later/id1060761517?i=1000658084188.

5. "Some South Africans Are Rethinking Nelson Mandela's Legacy," *Economist*, April 25, 2019, https://www.economist.com/special-report/2019/04/25/some-south-africans-are-rethinking-nelson-mandelas-legacy.

6. Theodore Stanton biography, Olympedia, https://www.olympedia.org/athletes/899345.

7. Elizabeth Cady Stanton, *Eighty Years and More: Reminiscences 1815-1897*, Chapter V: "Our Wedding Journey," https://digital.library.upenn.edu/women/stanton/years/years.html#V.

8. Marita Vlachou, "Van Jones Slams Double Standard Between Harris and Trump," *Huffpost*, October 24, 2024, https://www.huffpost.com/entry/van-jones-kamala-harris-donald-trump-comments_n_671a14b1e4b07a6807469694.

9. Adam Roberts, "Did Sexism Propel Donald Trump to Power?" *Economist Today* (email newsletter), November 10, 2024.

10. Richard Reeves, "Boosting Men Doesn't Come at Women's Expense," *Boston Globe*, November 13, 2024, https://www.bostonglobe.com/2024/11/13/opinion/election-gender-gap-richard-reeves/?p1=SectionFront_Feed_ContentQuery&p1=SectionFront_Feed_ContentQuery.

11. The phrase "a terrible beauty" comes from William Butler Yeats's poem, "Easter, 1916," in which he describes the Easter uprising against British rule in Ireland. "All changed, changed utterly: A terrible beauty is born," has been discussed by artists and historians ever since Yeats wrote those lines. "A terrible beauty" has also been used to describe natural wonders, inventions, marriages, and nations. I called the United States a terrible beauty because of the contrast between American ideals and realities, disappointments, and triumphs.

12. Cynthia Enloe, *The Big Push: Exposing and Challenging the Persistence of Patriarchy* (Oakland: University of California Press, 2017), 77.

CHAPTER ONE

1. Gerda Lerner Quotes > Quotable Quote, Goodreads, https://www.goodreads.com/quotes/10257580-first-of-all-nobody-gave-us-anything-it-makes-me.

2. Sonia Sodha, " 'White Feminists' Are Under Attack from Other Women. There Can Be Only One Winner—Men," *Guardian*, September 26, 2021, https://www.theguardian.com/commentisfree/2021/sep/26/white-feminists-are-under-attack-from-other-women-here-can-only-be-one-winner--men.

3. "Audre Lorde > Quotes," Goodreads, https://www.goodreads.com/author/quotes/18486.Audre_Lorde. I wonder what Audre Lorde, the great pioneering intersectional feminist, would have thought about the trashing of white suffragists in the twenty-first century. I suspect her views would be like those of Sonia Sodha. She voiced her great "Your silence will not protect you" quote in *Sister Outsider*, in an essay where she was encouraging Black women to stand up to Black men's sexism. She also said, "I am not free while any woman is unfree, even when her shackles are very different from my own."

4. Marsha Blackburn, Cindy Hyde-Smith, Cynthia Lummis, and Katie Britt, "This Monument Has Been Missing from the Mall Far Too Long," *Washington Post*, March 28, 2024, https://www.washingtonpost.com/opinions/2024/03/28/monument-american-women-national-mall/.

5.   Lisa Tetrault, *The Myth of Seneca Falls: Memory and the Women's Suffrage Movement, 1848-1898* (Chapel Hill: University of North Carolina Press, 2014), 188-190.

6.   Ibid., 196-197.

7.   During the Portrait Monument campaign, Patricia Schroeder's quip was extensively repeated—and this was in the days before social media. However, I can't find it in any books or websites. Nevertheless, those of us who were around during the campaign remember it well.

8.   Tetrault, *Myth of Seneca Falls*, 197.

9.   National Votes for Women Trail, https://ncwhs.org/votes-for-women-trail/.

10.   National Votes for Women Trail database, https://ncwhs.org/votes-for-women-trail/#trail.

11.   Brent Staples, "How the Suffrage Movement Betrayed Black Women," *New York Times,* July 18, 2018, https://www.nytimes.com/2018/07/28/opinion/sunday/suffrage-movement-racism-black-women.html.

12.   Never forget Otto von Bismarck's quip: "Two things people should not see being made, sausage and laws." Yes, Bismarck was an authoritarian, and I am not one of his fans, but I still laugh at his great remark.

13.   Staples, "How the Suffrage Movement."

14.   Staples, "How the Suffrage Movement," comments section, https://www.nytimes.com/2018/07/28/opinion/sunday/suffrage-movement-racism-black-women.html#commentsContainer.

15.   Ibid.

16.   Ibid.

17.   Coline Jenkins, "Opinion—Letters—The Suffragists and Their Descendants," *New York Times*, August 2, 2018, https://www.nytimes.com/2018/08/02/opinion/letters/racism-suffrage-movement.html.

18.   Ibid.

19.   Here is an example of a Pomeroy women's suffrage marker, https://www.hmdb.org/m.asp?m=224029. For more information on how to find the Pomeroy markers, read Theresa Dintino's article, "National Votes for Women Trail and Pomeroy Markers: Maybe There Is One in Your Town," https://www.nastywomenwriters.com/national-votes-for-women-trail-and-pomeroy-markers-maybe-there-is-one-in-your-town/.

20.   Millermore is a famous, supposedly haunted antebellum mansion. It is part of a historical park that was called Dallas Heritage Village in 2019 and 2020. The name has since changed to Old City Park. Barry Miller lived with his family at Millermore.

21.   In 1918, Nona Boren Mahoney, vice president of the Dallas Equal Suffrage Association, gathered ten thousand signatures within two weeks from a wide cross-section of Dallas women—wealthy, middle and working class, Protestant, Catholic, and Jewish—on a women's suffrage petition. It helped convince Dallas Sen. Barry Miller, an outspoken opponent of the Ku Klux Klan, to not only change his mind about women voting but to eventually lead the Women's Suffrage Caucus in the state House of Representatives. Unfortunately, all the women in the petition were white, but for its time and place, a petition with Catholic, Jewish, and working-class signatures was a major step forward, especially since Dallas was a Ku Klux Klan stronghold.

22.   NYT Editorial Board, "The 19th Amendment: An Important Milestone in an Unfinished Journey," *New York Times*, August 15, 2020, https://www.nytimes.com/2020/08/15/opinion/19th-amendment-centennial-suffrage.html?smid=tw-share/.

23.   Ibid.

24.   NYT Editorial Board, "The 19th Amendment," comments section.

25.   Ibid.

26.   Ibid.

27.   Ibid.

28.   Myriam Miedzian, "The Suffragists Were Not Racists, So Cancel the Cancel Culture and Celebrate an Accusation-Free Suffrage Centennial," myriammiedzian.com, August 19, 2020, https://www.myriammiedzian.com/suffragists-were-not-racists.

29.   Ellen Goodman and Lynn Sherr, "The Mother of All Celebrations," billmoyers.com, August 20, 2020, https://billmoyers.com/story/the-mother-of-all-celebrations/.

The title of this article should have never been "The Mother of All Celebrations," especially since the authors provide much evidence that the Nineteenth Amendment Centennial was a box office flop.

30.   Ibid.

31.   Staples, "How the Suffrage Movement," comments section, https://www.nytimes.com/2018/07/28/opinion/sunday/suffrage-movement-racism-black-women.html#commentsContainer.

32.   I currently attend a United Methodist church that uses an inclusive language translation of John 15:13, respected by most Bible scholars. But in the late 1960s, the only translations we had were the sexist ones. I do not think we should hide sexist, racist, classist, and homophobic language in old plays, operas, and literature because I want people to see how acceptable these -isms were in the past, and why social justice movements were so necessary.

33.   Cory Booker (username corybooker), comments about Alice Paul, Instagram, May 16, 2022, https://www.instagram.com/tv/CdoFLHQsnGK/.

34.   Amelia R. Fry, "Conversations with Alice Paul: Woman Suffrage and the Equal Rights Amendment," (Regents of the University of California, 1976), sec. 231. https://oac.cdlib.org/view?docId=kt6f59n89c&doc.view=entire_text.

35.   Leila J. Rupp and Verta Taylor, *Survival in the Doldrums: The American Women's Rights Movement, 1945 to the 1960s* (New York: Oxford University Press, 1987), 159. Some historians claim Alice Paul was anti-Semitic. Rupp and Taylor base their assertion on the comments of her friend, Mabel Vernon, who noted Paul's "antagonism for Jews." However, Rupp and Taylor never mentioned Paul's hard work in helping Jewish refugees escape to the United States. Rupp and Taylor generally take a dim view of Paul's suffrage and ERA activism, which led me to believe that she didn't do much for women's rights. However, after I saw Alice Paul's brilliance and heroism in *Iron Jawed Angels* and did more research, I realized that she was a great activist. Yes, she had her flaws—just like everyone else.

In recent years, several people have pushed back on the view that Paul hated Jews. See Hilary Danailova, "Jewish Suffragists, White Dresses, and Yellow Roses," *Hadassah*, July 2020, comments section: https://www.hadassahmagazine.org/2020/07/01/jewish-suffragists-white-dresses-yellow-roses/. Ruth Radesky told Danailova, "Alice Paul took my German Jewish refugee family into her home/office in Geneva in (I think) 1939 or 1940 and made them welcome and valued members of her community. She was instrumental in one Jewish family's surviving with some dignity. My grandmother always spoke of her with love and gratitude. You should not make the assertion that Paul was a 'notorious anti-semite' without evidence."

36.   Alice Paul Center for Gender Justice, "Who was Alice Paul? Feminist. Suffragist. Political Strategist," https://www.alicepaul.org/about-alice-paul/.

37.   For an example of the Code of Conduct, see "Supreme Court Preview," Alice Paul Institute, https://www.youtube.com/watch?v=BN-1M6WhPgM.

38.   Alice Paul Center for Gender Justice, "Alice Paul Center Makes Its Debut," October 1, 2024, https://www.alicepaul.org/alice-paul-center-for-gender-justice-makes-its-debut/. Even after API morphed into the Alice Paul Center, the staff still didn't get over the "gave women the vote" habit. The page says, "which gave some women the right to vote," and "The 19th did give the right to vote to all women, but which women specifically was an issue left to the states . . . ."

39.   Alice Paul Center for Gender Justice, "About the Alice Paul Center," https://www.alicepaul.org/about-the-institute/.

40.   Rachael Glashan Rupisan, "Paulsdale Tour," email message to Joanne Callahan, October 11, 2024.

41.   Ibid.

42.   Joanne Callahan, "Re: Paulsdale Tour," email message to Rachael Glashan Rupisan, October 11, 2024.

43.   Detransitioning is a sensitive topic and is often viewed as a smoke screen for transphobia. However, Robin Respaut, Chad Terhune, and Michelle Conlin argue that "understanding the reasons some transgender people quit treatment is key to improving it." See "Why Detransitioners Are Crucial to the Science of Gender Care," *Reuters*, December 22, 2022: https://www.reuters.com/investigates/special-report/usa-transyouth-outcomes/.

44.   Rachael Glashan Rupisan—Alice Paul Center, fundraising letter to Joanne Callahan, November 30, 2024.

45.   Ibid.

46.   J. D. Zahniser and Amelia R. Fry, *Alice Paul: Claiming Power* (New York: Oxford University Press, 2014), 23.

47.   Pat Loeb, "As a Leading Force in Women's Suffrage, Why Is South Jersey Native Alice Paul Largely Forgotten?" KYW Newsradio 1060, August 21, 2020, https://www.audacy.com/kywnewsradio/articles/feature-article/why-is-crucial-suffragist-alice-paul-largely-forgotten.

48.   Alice Paul Center, "Who Was Alice Paul?"

49.   Marguerite Kearns, "News of US Suffrage Martyr Inez Milholland Has Been Spreading," Inez Milholland Centennial, https://inezmilhollandcentennial.com/index.html.

50. Inez Milholland Centennial, 2016 nomination for the Presidential Citizens Medal, https://inezmilhollandcentennial.com/inez.html.

51. Ibid.

52. Ibid.

53. Ibid.

54. Ibid.

55. Marguerite Kearns, "Inez Milholland Honored at Her Grave in Lewis, NY, during January's Women's March!" suffragewagon.org, February 10, 2017, https://www.suffragewagon.org/inez-milholland-honored-at-her-grave-in-lewis-ny-during-januarys-womens-march/.

56. Jeanine Michna-Bales, *Standing Together: Inez Milholland's Final Campaign for Women's Suffrage* (New York: MW Editions, 2021), 13.

57. Women's Congressional Policy Institute, "House Honors Alice Paul, Pioneer of Women's Suffrage Movement," https://www.wcpinst.org/source/house-honors-alice-paul-pioneer-of-womens-suffrage-movement/.

58. Marie Solis, "The Decades-Long Debate Over Whether Women Vote Like Their Husbands," *Vice*, August 3, 2020, https://www.vice.com/en/article/the-decades-long-debate-over-whether-women-vote-like-their-husbands/.

59. Alana Valko, "Some Conservative Men Don't Believe Men Silence Women's Votes at the Polls—These 18 Stories Are Proving Otherwise," *Buzzfeed*, November 4, 2024, https://www.buzzfeed.com/alanavalko/women-voter-suppression-men-husband.

60. Ibid.

61. Solis, "Decades-Long Debate."

62. Kristin Brey, "Married Women Could Face New Obstacles to Vote. This Is What Conservatives Want," *USA Today*, February 22, 2025, https://currently.att.yahoo.com/news/married-women-could-face-obstacles-100648540.html.

63. Scott Bomboy, "The Vote That Led to the 19th Amendment," National Constitution Center, August 18, 2023, https://constitutioncenter.org/blog/the-man-and-his-mom-who-gave-women-the-vote.

64. Bill Haltom, *Joseph Hanover & the Suffragents* (video), Alice Paul Institute, April 19, 2021, https://www.youtube.com/watch?v=4v0pMcZTYTo.

65. Bridget Quinn, "The Eastern European Jewish Immigrant Who Saved

Suffrage," Forward, August 18, 2020, https://forward.com/culture/452813/tennessee-ratifies-19th-amendment-joe-hanover-jewish-immigrant-harry-burn/.

66.   I almost called Austin a blue island in a sea of red but changed my mind because in 1919, red was the color of communism, and the children of American communists were called red-diaper babies. It's funny to think that a color that used to symbolize the extreme left in this country is now the color of conservatism.

67.   Taylor Stewart, "Biographical Sketch of Lucille Shields," Alexander Street: Part of Clarivate (website), 2024, https://documents.alexanderstreet.com/d/1008297964.

68.   Cassondra St. Cyr, Anne Peterson, and Taylor Franks, "The National Woman's Party—Chapter 4: Victory!" Mapping American Social Movements Project, https://depts.washington.edu/moves/NWP_project_ch4.shtml. The Watchfire demonstrations were controversial because NWP protestors burned copies of Wilson's speeches. They were deeply frustrated with Wilson making pro-democracy speeches at home and abroad but not encouraging the US Senate to ratify the Nineteenth Amendment. They carried banners with messages such as "President Wilson is deceiving the world when he appears as the prophet of democracy." In one instance, they burned a two-foot Wilson in effigy; he was a small doll stuffed with straw. The Watchfire demonstrations were the closest the suffragists had come to using violence. However, reactions to the Watchfire demonstrations were far more violent than the demonstrations themselves.

69.   Melissa Kean, "Elizabeth Kalb, '16: The Owl Who Beat Texas," Rice History Corner, October 11, 2016, https://ricehistorycorner.com/2016/10/11/elizabeth-kalb-16-the-owl-who-beat-texas/.

70.   Catherine M. Cilfone, "Snell Wolfe Homeowner Says Sign Too Big," email message to Joanne Callahan, Denise Ireton, Erin Hegberg, and Sehila Mota Casper, August 12, 2020.

71.   If I had known I was going to write this book, I would have taken notes when I called the Bullock Museum and spoke to the curator of the Texas women's suffrage exhibit. I have forgotten the exact date when I called and I don't remember the curator's name, but I am not making anything up when I say I made the call. It certainly wouldn't do me any good if I lied about something like that.

72.   "Jailed for Freedom," Bullock Texas State History Museum, https://www.thestoryoftexas.com/discover/artifacts/jailed-for-freedom.

73.   Michael Agresta, "How Texas Women Delivered the Nineteenth

Amendment," *Texas Observer*, August 17, 2020, https://www.texasobserver.org/nineteenth-amendment-centennial-texas-women/.

74. Joanne Callahan, "Your Coverage of the Texas Women's Suffrage Movement," email message to editors of the *Texas Observer*, August 24, 2020. I acknowledged that the article made several good points but said it was wrong to omit the NWP. I said that to do justice to the Texas Women's Suffrage Movement, the *Texas Observer* needed to post at least three in-depth articles: the mainstream movement; Texas and the NWP; and Latina, African American, and Native American suffragists.

75. Nancy Schiesari, *Citizens at Last: Texas Women Fight for the Vote,* Public Broadcasting System (PBS), 2021, https://www.citizensatlastfilm.com/. Overall, *Citizens at Last* was a very good documentary. Unlike the dull exhibit on Texas women's suffrage at the Texas State Fair in 2017, the documentary had great historical footage; it was frank about Texas patriarchy and the impact of the Jim Crow laws; it paid homage to African American and Hispanic activists; it didn't ignore Alice Paul and her powerful impact on the movement; it quoted the misogynistic and racist statements of Texas state legislators word for word; and it showed why Annette Finnigan, Jane Yelvington McCallum, and especially Minnie Fisher Cunningham and Carrie Chapman Catt were such great leaders. But ignoring Clara Snell Wolfe, Lucille Shields, and Elizabeth Kalb is a major omission, and it is not good enough just to say a few words about Alice Paul.

76. Shirley M. Marshall, *A Radical Suffragist in Washington, D.C.: An Inside Story of the National Woman's Party* (Charleston, SC: The History Press, 2024), 132.

77. Ibid., 137.

78. Agresta, "How Texas Women Delivered."

79. Marshall, *A Radical Suffragist,* 143.

80. Ibid., preface (no page numbers are listed in the preface).

81. Ibid., 143-146.

82. Janet L. Yellen, "The History of Women's Work and Wages and How It Has Created Success for Us All," Brookings Institution, May 2020, https://www.brookings.edu/articles/the-history-of-womens-work-and-wages-and-how-it-has-created-success-for-us-all/. Yellen says that 5 percent of married women were in the labor force. However, other economists say it was closer to 12 percent. Yellen implies that those statistics may have excluded women of color. Black and Hispanic married women often worked as housekeepers and nannies; several did factory and agricultural work. Yellen also hints that the statistics do not count the types

of paid labor that married women usually performed: co-managing mom-and-pop shops, renting rooms in their house to boarders, and working in their homes as seamstresses, bakers, and childcare workers to make a little extra money. But those "mom jobs" are different from running your own business or working full time for a corporation. Benigna Green Kalb was a pioneering businesswoman.

83.   Ibid., 145-146.

84.   Ibid., 165.

85.   Ibid., 8.

86.   Ibid., 134.

87.   Michele Stopera Freyhauf, "Lucy Burns: A Look at a Catholic American Suffragette," Feminism and Religion (website), September 20, 2012, https://feminismandreligion.com/2012/09/20/lucy-burns-catholic-suffrage-freyhauf/.

88.   Hollis Walker, "Karen Kedrowski: Carrie Chapman Catt and the 19th Amendment," *Durango Herald*, August 26, 2020, https://www.durangoherald.com/articles/karen-kedrowski-carrie-chapman-catt-and-the-19th-amendment/.

89.   Lucy Burns, Wikipedia, https://en.wikipedia.org/wiki/Lucy_Burns.

90.   Kelly Marino, "We 'Protest the Unjust Treatment of Pickets': Brooklyn Suffragist Lucy Burns, Militancy in the National Woman's Party, and Prison Reform, 1917–1920," *Long Island History Journal*, Volume 2801, 2020. https://lihj.cc.stonybrook.edu/2020/articles/we-protest-the-unjust-treatment-of-pickets-brooklyn-suffragist-lucy-burns-militancy-in-the-national-womans-party-and-prison-reform-1917-1920/.

91.   Ibid.

92.   Zahniser and Fry, *Alice Paul: Claiming Power*, 318, Kindle Edition.

93.   Marino, "We 'Protest the Unjust Treatment.' "

94.   Amelia R. Fry, "Conversations with Alice Paul: Woman Suffrage and the Equal Rights Amendment," (Regents of the University of California, 1976), sec. 257 (What Next? Lucy Burns), https://oac.cdlib.org/view?docId=kt6f59n89c&doc.view=entire_text.

95.   Marino, "We 'Protest the Unjust Treatment.' "

96.   David Smith, "Ida B. Wells: The Great Unsung Heroine of the Civil Rights Movement," *Guardian*, April 27, 2018, https://www.theguardian.com/world/2018/apr/27/ida-b-wells-civil-rights-movement-reporter.

97.   W. E. B. Du Bois, "On Stalin," March 16, 1953, https://www.marxists.org/reference/archive/stalin/biographies/1953/03/16.htm. Du Bois starts his essay with, "Joseph Stalin was a great man." He is silent about Stalin's purge trials. Most online articles about Paul Robeson and Du Bois struggle with those blind spots on Stalin because the authors admire both men so much. It's just more evidence of giving "great men" a pass on their huge mistakes.

98.   Jamie Shelton, "The Rosa Parks House—at Home in Berlin? A Talk by Kristin Kopp, Ph.D.," *Bates Student*, March 6, 2024, https://thebatesstudent.com/25581/news/the-rosa-parks-house-at-home-in-berlin-a-talk-by-kristin-kopp-ph-d/. Fascinating article about the movement to preserve Rosa Parks's Detroit house and find a permanent place for it. Currently, the house resides in Berlin.

99.   Maud Sampson Williams was the founder and president of the El Paso Negro Woman's Civic and Equal Franchise League.

She led a successful voter registration drive for African American women at the El Paso County Courthouse in July 1918. She also led the campaign to admit her suffrage league into both the Texas Equal Suffrage Association and NAWSA as an auxiliary member. But it was rejected because most white suffragist leaders feared that a women's suffrage amendment would never make it into the Constitution if their organizations were integrated, even on an auxiliary basis.

Maud Sampson Williams was one of the founders of the Phillis Wheatley Club of El Paso. She was also vice president of the El Paso chapter of the NAACP from 1917 to 1924 and chaired its Legal Redress Committee in the 1950s. Her committee attempted to desegregate Texas Western College, now the University of Texas at El Paso, shortly after the *Brown v. Board of Education* Supreme Court decision. Williams accompanied Thelma Joyce White, the valedictorian of Douglass School in 1954, to Texas Western to help her register for classes. White was denied admission, which led to *White v. Smith* (1955), the US District Court decision that ultimately desegregated the college.

Maud Sampson Williams's birth name was Maud Craig. She married Edward D. Sampson in 1907, a marriage that lasted until his death in 1926. She married Emerson Williams in 1929, and he died in 1947. Maud Sampson Williams was killed in 1958 in a pedestrian traffic accident in Oklahoma City.

100.   Fry, "Conversations with Alice Paul," secs. 343 and 344.

101.   On weekdays, you can go to the Washington, DC, L'Enfant Plaza station and take the Virginia Railway Express (VRE) to the VRE Lorton station. After you arrive at VRE Lorton, you can take a short Uber or Lyft to the Turning Point memorial.

CHAPTER TWO

1.   Goodman and Sherr, "Mother of All Celebrations."

2.   Ibid.

3.   Susan Faludi, "American Electra: Feminism's Ritual Matricide," susanfaludi.com, October 2010, https://susanfaludi.com/americanelectra.pdf.

4.   Kim Willsher, "Anne Hidalgo: 'I Am Who I Am. I Don't Play a Role,' " *Guardian*, June 23, 2014, https://www.theguardian.com/lifeandstyle/2014/jun/23/anne-hidalgo-first-female-mayor-paris-interview. French conservatives say that if a mayor is a woman, we should still address her in the masculine as *Madame Le Maire*. However, many French people, including Anne Hidalgo herself, are rejecting that tradition and addressing women mayors in the feminine as *Madame La Maire*.

5.   Michael Brune, "Pulling Down Our Monuments," Sierra Club (website), July 22, 2020. Comments are towards the end of the article. https://www.sierraclub.org/michael-brune/2020/07/john-muir-early-history-sierra-club.

6.   "Sierra Club v. John Muir," John Muir Global Network, https://johnmuir.org/sierra-club-vs-john-muir/.

7.   Donald Worster, "John Muir Biographer: He Was No White Supremacist," *California Sun*, July 29, 2020, https://www.californiasun.co/john-muir-biographer-he-was-no-white-supremacist/.

8.   "Women's Suffrage, Historical Markers, and Race," National Collaborative for Women's History Sites, https://ncwhs.org/about/.

9.   "The 1920 election—The Nineteenth Amendment: The Fight for Women's Suffrage as Seen Through *The Woman Citizen*," Berkeley Library University of California, https://exhibits.lib.berkeley.edu/spotlight/women-vote/feature/the-1920-election.

10.   James FitzGerald, "Just How Big Was Donald Trump's Election Victory?" *BBC News*, November 23, 2024, https://www.bbc.com/news/articles/cn5w9w160xdo.

11.   Mark Lawrence Schrad, "Why Do We Blame Women for Prohibition?" *Politico Magazine*, January 13, 2019, https://www.politico.com/magazine/story/2019/01/13/prohibition-women-blame-history-223972/.

12.   "Women's Suffrage in Ohio," Wikipedia, https://en.wikipedia.org/wiki/Women%27s_suffrage_in_Ohio#cite_note-FOOTNOTEPliley200813-80.

Some suffragists distanced themselves as much as possible from the temperance movement, especially if they lived in the German Belt. While there were several outstanding German American suffragists, including Pauline Perlmutter Steinem (Gloria Steinem's grandmother), many German communities were against women's suffrage. They were suspicious of its association with the temperance movement; they thought most suffrage groups were too "Yankee Anglo-Saxon Protestant" and that they didn't like Germans; and above all, they believed that the husband is the head of the household.

13.   Episode Three of the Ken Burns-Lynn Novick documentary, *Prohibition*, has an extensive profile of Pauline Sabin and her powerful, 1.5 million-member anti-Prohibition organization.

14.   Miedzian, "Suffragists Were Not Racists."

15.   Martin Pengelly, "David Blight on Frederick Douglass: 'I Call Him Beautifully Human,' " *Guardian*, October 28, 2018, https://www.theguardian.com/books/2018/oct/28/david-blight-on-frederick-douglass-i-call-him-beautifully-human. Blight claims that he is not letting Douglass off the hook, but in his biography, he constantly reminds us that Douglass was a nineteenth century man. It felt like Blight was telling us, "Thou shalt always keep Frederick Douglass on a pedestal."

16.   Fry, "Conversations with Alice Paul," sec. 133.

17.   "9,000 Women Sign Protest on Hitler," *New York Times*, August 14, 1933, https://timesmachine.nytimes.com/timesmachine/1933/08/14/99918390.html?pageNumber=5. Among the famous women who signed the letter were Jane Addams, Charlotte Perkins Gilman, and Dr. Grace Abbott, director of the Federal Children's Bureau.

18.   Kalee Baucom, "Woolf on Hitler's Hit List," *Blogging Woolf* (blog), October 9, 2015, https://bloggingwoolf.org/2015/10/09/woolf-on-hitlers-hit-list/. Feminists Virginia Woolf and Vera Brittain were on Hitler's hit list of British people who would have been arrested if the Nazis had conquered Britain. Because of her peace and anti-Nazi activism, there is no doubt in my mind that Carrie Chapman Catt would have been arrested if the Nazis had taken over this country. Catt was already under FBI surveillance because of her leadership in anti-war organizations.

19.   Sonia Pressman Fuentes, "Legendary Feminist: Alice Paul," *Stories & Articles by Sonia*, 1998, http://www.erraticimpact.com/~feminism/html/FUENTES_articles_alice_paul.htm. Alice Paul's refugee work is described towards the lower middle section of the article.

20.   "Southern States Woman Suffrage Conference," Wikipedia, https://en.wikipedia.org/wiki/Southern_States_Woman_Suffrage_Conference#:~:text=The%20Southern%20States%20Woman%20Suffrage,white%20women%20of%20prominent%20families.

21.   Laurel Bower and Kathleen Grathwol, "To the Wrongs That Need Resistance—Carrie Chapman Catt's Lifelong Fight for Women's Suffrage," National Park Service, December 14, 2020, https://www.nps.gov/articles/000/to-the-wrongs-that-need-resistance-carrie-chapman-catt-s-lifelong-fight-for-women-s-suffrage.htm.

22.   Mat Smart, *The Agitators: The Story of Susan B. Anthony and Frederick Douglass* (podcast), Episode Six, National Park Service Women's History, https://www.nps.gov/subjects/womenshistory/the-agitators-episode-six.htm.

23.   A millennial friend thumbed her nose at those facts until I told her that in 1950s Hollywood, Richard Widmark had Sidney Poitier over to his house for dinner and police officers stopped Poitier outside the house until Widmark berated them. See "Richard Widmark Trivia" at https://www.imdb.com/name/nm0001847/trivia/.

24.   "Helen Pitts," *New World Encyclopedia*, https://www.newworldencyclopedia.org/entry/Helen_Pitts.

25.   Dianne Bystrom, "Consider Carrie Chapman Catt's Whole Life and Legacy," Bleeding Heartland (website), October 4, 2021, https://www.bleedingheartland.com/2021/10/04/consider-carrie-chapman-catts-whole-life-and-legacy/.

26.   Sharon Harley, "African American Women and the Nineteenth Amendment," National Park Service, April 10, 2019. https://www.nps.gov/articles/african-american-women-and-the-nineteenth-amendment.htm#_edn6.

27.   John Blake, "Did Black Lives Matter to Abraham Lincoln? It's Complicated," CNN, March 14, 2021, https://www.cnn.com/2021/03/14/us/abraham-lincoln-racism-blake/index.html.

My comments about the either/or proposition spring from this paragraph:

"But Jeffries' interpretation of Lincoln's racial views reflects our contemporary tendency to see racism as an either/or proposition: You're either a racist or a not. Lincoln was something else, and many still haven't caught up with the enigmatic man who David Blight, a leading Lincoln historian, calls 'a creature of contradictions and ambiguities.' "

28.   Isabela Salas-Betsch and Kate Kelly, "What Comes Next for the Equal

Rights Amendment?" americanprogress.org, August 26, 2024, https://www.americanprogress.org/article/what-comes-next-for-the-equal-rights-amendment/.

29.   When I have told people that American women could have easily ended up in the same situation as their French and Swiss sisters, I have usually gotten an eyeroll followed by an assertion that the French and Swiss are more "traditional." However, the French women's rights movement began during the French Revolution, when a group of women petitioned the National Assembly in November 1789 for equal rights and Olympe de Gouges wrote the groundbreaking Declaration of the Rights of Woman and the Female Citizen in 1791—almost sixty years before the women's rights convention in Seneca Falls. Arguably, the Swiss are more conservative than Americans, for their Women's Suffrage Movement started in 1868. Nevertheless, there has always been a strong, well-funded anti-feminist movement in this country, and they could have easily pulled a Switzerland on us.

30.   During the Pomeroy women's suffrage marker unveiling at Wooldridge Square in Austin in October 2022, Catherine Alvarado Cilfone gave a speech and said that her grandmother was one of the first women to vote in Victoria, Texas.

31.   "How Ida B. Wells Got Women Voting," *Smithsonian*, January 21, 2022, https://www.youtube.com/watch?v=hQsu0TGgjbs.

32.   Jennifer Harlan, "My ___ was a Suffragist," *New York Times*, August 19, 2020, https://www.nytimes.com/2020/07/02/style/woman-suffrage-movement-descend.html.

33.   Untitled article, *Clarksville Leaf-Chronicle*, November 29, 1920, page 4. The untitled article lists who voted, and it says that "two colored women voted."

34.   Robert Siegel, "When African American Voters Shifted Away from the GOP," National Public Radio (NPR), August 25, 2016, https://www.npr.org/2016/08/25/491389942/when-african-american-voters-shifted-away-from-the-gop.

35.   "New Coin Celebrates the Living Legacy of Ida B. Wells," Smithsonian American Women's History Museum, December 30, 2024, https://womenshistory.si.edu/blog/new-coin-celebrates-living-legacy-ida-b-wells.

36.   Mark Memmott, "Listen: Rare Recording of 1952 Speech That King Drew From," NPR, August 28, 2013, https://www.npr.org/sections/thetwo-way/2013/08/28/216466421/listen-rare-recording-of-52-speech-that-king-drew-from. It is obvious that King pulled some statements in his "I Have a Dream" speech from the Carey speech and that he should have given him credit. "I Have a Dream"

is a great speech, but we shouldn't excuse King's plagiarism and sexist language.

37.   "A Brief History of Civil Rights in the United States: 1965 Voting Rights Act," Howard University School of Law, January 6, 2023, https://library.law. howard.edu/civilrightshistory/blackrights/vra.

38.   Blake, "Did Black Lives Matter."

39.   Ibid.

40.   "The Vote: Part 1," *American Experience*, PBS, August 2020, https://www. pbs.org/wgbh/americanexperience/films/vote/.

41.   Ibid.

42.   Sojourner Truth, "Address to the First Annual Meeting of the American Equal Rights Association—May 9, 1867," Iowa State University Archives of Women's Political Communication, https://awpc.cattcenter.iastate.edu/2017/03/21/ address-to-the-first-annual-meeting-of-the-american-equal-rights-association- may-9-1867/.

43.   Smart, *The Agitators*.

44.   Peter Marks, "Two Heroes of 19th-Century America Seek Justice. They Get None in *The Agitators*," *Washington Post*, October 31, 2018, https://www. washingtonpost.com/entertainment/theater_dance/two-heroes-of-19th-century- america-seek-justice-they-get-none-in-the-agitators/2018/10/31/2b71efb4-dd06- 11e8-b732-3c72cbf131f2_story.html.

45.   Ibid. Comments section.

46.   Ibid. Comments section.

47.   "Women's Loyal National League," Wikipedia, https://en.wikipedia.org/ wiki/Women%27s_Loyal_National_League.

48.   Ibid.

49.   "Address from the Women's Loyal National League Supporting the Abolition of Slavery," DocsTeach, January 25, 1864, https://www.docsteach.org/documents/ document/address-womens-loyal-national-league.

50.   Jennifer Szalai, "A Big New Biography Treats Frederick Douglass as Man, Not Myth," *New York Times*, October 17, 2018, https://www.nytimes. com/2018/10/17/books/review-frederick-douglass-prophet-of-freedom-david- blight.html. Because Ottilie Assing had breast cancer when she committed suicide, some biographers don't think Douglass's marriage to Helen Pitts had anything to do with it. However, the combination of breast cancer and Douglass's

marriage may have provoked so much despair that she took her own life.

51. Susan Ware, "Carrie & Mollie & Anna & Lucy: Queering the Women's Suffrage Movement," PBS, October 23, 2020, https://www.pbs.org/wgbh/americanexperience/features/vote-carrie-mollie-anna-lucy/. The documentary itself did not talk about the queer women in the movement. However, on The Vote website, there were several supplemental articles about the movement.

52. "Transcript: Ezra Klein Interviews Michelle Goldberg," *Ezra Klein Show*, *New York Times*, July 8, 2022, https://www.nytimes.com/2022/07/08/podcasts/transcript-ezra-klein-interviews-michelle-goldberg.html.

53. Faludi, "American Electra." Marie Wilson calls generational conflicts the San Andreas Fault of feminism.

54. Ibid.

55. Ibid. The quote about republican motherhood came from Linda Kerber.

56. Ibid.

57. Judith Warner, Emily Baxter, and Milia Fisher, "4 Generations of American Women: Great Progress, Persistent Challenges," Center for American Progress, May 12, 2015, https://www.americanprogress.org/wp-content/uploads/sites/2/2015/05/4generations-brief.pdf.

58. Rupisan, fundraising letter.

59. Nancy Folbre, *The Invisible Heart: Economics and Family Values* (New York: The New Press, 2001), 73.

60. Faludi, "American Electra."

61. National Women's History Alliance homepage, https://nationalwomenshistoryalliance.org/.

62. To guard against historical malpractice, the suffragists probably would have written autobiographies, given more interviews, written their own history books, and worked hard to become savvy at dealing with journalists and historians.

CHAPTER THREE

1. Jessica Bennett and Veronica Chambers, "Suffrage Isn't 'Boring History.' It's a Story of Political Geniuses," *New York Times*, August 19, 2020, https://www.nytimes.com/2020/07/10/us/women-voting-rights-suffrage-centennial.html.

2.   Anita Sarkeesian and Laura Hudson, "We Must Rewrite Women's Role in History," *Time Magazine*, March 8, 2016, https://time.com/4248910/women-in-history/.

3.   Rebecca Traister, Quotes, Goodreads, https://www.goodreads.com/quotes/9726224-the-ability-to-feel-the-anger-and-convey-it-to.

4.   In america250.org, I saw Civil Rights Movement pictures but nothing, absolutely nothing, about women's suffrage and feminism.

5.   "Most People Opposed Women's Suffrage," New York Heritage Digital Collections, https://nyheritage.org/exhibits/recognizing-womens-right-vote-new-york-state/most-people-opposed-womens-suffrage.

6.   Soraya Chemaly, "Women's Equality Day Is Meaningless to Most People, but That's Not an Accident," *Role Reboot*, August 26, 2015, http://www.rolereboot.org/culture-and-politics/details/2015-08-womens-equality-day-is-meaningless-to-most-people-but-thats-not-an-accident/index.html.

7.   Ibid.

8.   Zawn Villines, "Sexism Is the Core Problem in Most Heterosexual Relationships," *Liberating Motherhood* (blog), September 12, 2024, https://zawn.substack.com/p/sexism-is-the-core-problem-in-most.

9.   David J. Ayers, "The Cohabitation Dilemma Comes for America's Pastors," *Christianity Today*, April 2021, https://www.christianitytoday.com/2021/03/cohabitation-dilemma-comes-for-american-pastors-ayers/. Surprising article about the large number of evangelicals who cohabit before marriage.

10.   Amalfi Parker Elder, Esq., and Patrice Tillery, "Black Women, a History of Creating Our Own Spaces," BWJP, February 19, 2024, https://bwjp.org/black-women-a-history-of-creating-our-own-spaces/.

11.   *The Vote*, Part 2, *American Experience*, PBS, August 2020, https://www.pbs.org/wgbh/americanexperience/films/vote/.

12.   "Andrea Villarreal Gonzalez and Teresa Villarreal Gonzalez: Labor and Women's Rights Activists," page two, Museo del Westside, https://www.museodelwestside.org/women-activism/andrea-and-teresa-villarreal.

13.   Anna Laymon, "The Feminist History of 'Take Me Out to the Ball Game,'" *Smithsonian Magazine*, July 14, 2020, https://www.smithsonianmag.com/history/feminist-history-take-me-out-ball-game-180973307/.

14.   *The Vote*, Part 2.

15.   Ibid.

16.   Ibid.

17.   Ibid.

18.   Ibid.

19.   Marguerite Kearns, *An Unfinished Revolution: Edna Buckman Kearns and the Struggle for Women's Rights* (Albany: State University of New York Press, 2021). The book should have been subtitled, *The Love Story of Edna Buckman and Wilbur Kearns*.

20.   "The Anti-Wedding of Lucy Stone and Henry Blackwell," New England Historical Society, https://newenglandhistoricalsociety.com/anti-wedding-lucy-stone-and-henry-blackwell/.

21.   Paula Casey, who was mentored by Carol Lynn Yellin, gave me that quote in a personal conversation in the spring of 2023. I haven't found the quote anywhere on the internet.

22.   Harlan, "My ___ was a Suffragist."

23.   Vivian Anderson Castleberry, *Daughters of Dallas: A History of Greater Dallas Through the Voices and Deeds of Its Women*, (Dallas: Odenwald Press, 1994), 242-244.

24.   Searching for the Seneca Falls 100 (website), 2025, https://www.100signersproject.com/. Fascinating website about the lives of the sixty-eight women and thirty-two men who signed the Declaration of Sentiments.

25.   Doris Stevens, "Appendix 4: Suffrage Prisoners," in *Jailed for Freedom*, https://chswg.binghamton.edu/WASM-US/crowdsourcing/Stevens_JailedForFreedom_Appendix4.pdf. Several descriptions give information about the prisoners' ancestry.

26.   Joan Bradley Wages, "Women, their rights, and nothing less," mass email sent by National Women's History Museum to Joanne Callahan, October 26, 2016.

27.   Joanne Goodwin and C. M. Marihugh, "S01E05 Nevada: Prospecting for Voters in the Silver State," *Her March to Democracy: National Votes for Women Trail* (podcast), March 15, 2024, https://hermarchtodemocracy.buzzsprout.com/2283722/episodes/14613905-s01-e05-nevada-prospecting-for-voters-in-the-silver-state?t=0.

28.   *The Vote*, Part 2.

29.   Caroline Carrico, "Equality Trailblazers Monument: 'A Gift to the City,'" *Storyboard Memphis*, July 4, 2022. https://storyboardmemphis.org/history/equality-trailblazers-monument/.

30.   Katha Pollitt, "Feminist Mothers, Flapper Daughters?" *Nation*, September 30, 2010. https://www.thenation.com/article/archive/feminist-mothers-flapper-daughters/

31.   Carrico, "Equality Trailblazers Monument."

32.   Ibid.

33.   Ibid.

34.   Linda T. Wynn, "Profiles of African Americans in Tennessee: Mattie Coleman," Nashville Conference on African American History and Culture, 2011. https://digitalscholarship.tnstate.edu/cgi/viewcontent.cgi?article=1042&context=conference-on-african-american-history-and-culture.

35.   Caroline Sanders Clements, "How a Nashville Landmark Played a Part in Women's Suffrage," *Garden & Gun*, August 18, 2020, https://gardenandgun.com/articles/how-a-nashville-landmark-played-a-part-in-womens-suffrage/.

36.   Sophie Bolich, "New Beer Honors Women's Rights Advocate Mathilde Anneke," *Urban Milwaukee*, July 10, 2024, https://urbanmilwaukee.com/2024/07/10/new-beer-honors-womens-rights-advocate-mathilde-anneke/. Hillary Clinton needs to get together with the producers of that fine trilogy of German TV dramas about Berlin's famous Charité hospital, *Charité, Charité at War,* and *Charité Cold War,* and co-produce a series about Mathilde Anneke. Her life was a movie. All sorts of drama followed her wherever she went. I would like for Clinton and the *Charité* producers to work on the Anneke TV series because all the *Charité* shows had strong, pioneering female protagonists.

37.   "Susan B. Anthony," *Saturday Night Live*, January 14, 2017, https://www.youtube.com/watch?v=ZnpMeNyX3mg.

38.   "Susan B. Anthony House Clears Up Misconception," *News 10 NBC*, January 19, 2017 https://www.youtube.com/watch?v=uzubC1iEYQA.

39.   Victoria Brzustowicz, "Interpreting Susan B. Anthony for Our Times," Susan B. Anthony Museum and House, March 21, 2018, https://susanb.org/tag/saturday-night-live/.

40.   Harper D. Ward, "Misrepresenting Susan B. Anthony on Abortion," Susan B. Anthony Museum and House, 2018, https://susanbanthonyhouse.org/blog/misrepresenting-susan-b-anthony-on-abortion/.

41.   Caroline Kitchener, "Was Susan B. Anthony Antiabortion? Two Sides Are Dueling over the Answer—and the Definition of Feminism," *Washington Post*,

July 30, 2020, https://www.washingtonpost.com/gender-identity/was-susan-b-anthony-antiabortion-two-sides-are-dueling-over-the-answer-and-the-definition-of-feminism/.

42.　Ibid.

43.　Ibid.

44.　Ibid.

45.　Ibid.

46.　Ibid.

47.　The title, Log Cabin Republicans, implicitly pays homage to Lincoln as a Republican leader who believed in liberty and justice. Even though Log Cabin Republicans is a support group for LGBTIQ+ Republicans, it is silent about the controversy over Lincoln's sexual orientation. I couldn't find any statements about the issue on its website. Log Cabin Republicans is appealing to Republican pride as the party of Lincoln, quite different from asserting that he was gay or bisexual. Thus, we can use his name to promote LGBTIQ+ candidates and policies.

48.　"Susan B. Inspires Me Campaign," susanb.org, https://www.expansion.susanb.org/.

49.　Because of the dark lighting, glaring glass, and black background, I couldn't get a good picture of the Susan B. Anthony display on my iPhone. Nevertheless, Anthony was not a protégé or student of Douglass. They had a long, but stormy, friendship.

50.　Ann D. Gordon, *Was Susan B. Anthony a Racist?* (video), Susan B. Anthony birthday luncheon, 2017, Susan B. Anthony Museum and House, https://susanb.org/susan-b-anthony-and-racism/.

51.　Linda Lopata, "If Susan B. Anthony Was Racist," Susan B. Anthony Museum and House, https://susanb.org/if-susan-b-anthony-was-racist/.

52.　Myriam Miedzian, "The Shaming Must Stop: Elizabeth Cady Stanton and Susan B. Anthony Are American Heroes," myriammiedzian.com, 2021, https://www.myriammiedzian.com/shaming-must-stop.

53.　Karen M. Kedrowski, "Getting It Right: Carrie Chapman Catt," *Medium*, March 3, 2020, https://medium.com/iowa-history/getting-it-right-carrie-chapman-catt-579863d973cd.

54.　Ibid.

55.　Ibid.

56.   "Considering of Removing Names from University Property," Iowa State University Policy Library, November 25, 2020, https://www.policy.iastate.edu/policy/unnaming.

57.   *Catt Hall Review—Initial Report*, August 31, 2023, Iowa State University, https://iastate.app.box.com/s/kqe216kd1z8j5vrfs4kijo4jhaictur0.

58.   Brian Meyer, "Initial Vote Supports Catt's Name on Building," Iowa State University—Inside Iowa State for Faculty and Staff, August 31, 2023, https://www.inside.iastate.edu/article/2023/08/31/catt.

59.   Jay Waagmeester, "Carrie on: Catt Hall Will Keep Name, Committee Concludes," *Iowa State Daily*, November 9, 2023, https://iowastatedaily.com/285015/news/catt-hall-will-keep-name/.

60.   Ibid., 25-26, 29-33.

61.   Ibid., 30.

62.   Ibid., 31.

63.   Ibid., 21.

64.   Ibid., 27.

65.   Ibid., 28.

66.   Ibid., 20.

67.   Ibid., 21.

68.   *Catt Hall Review—Public Comments*, Iowa State University, November 9, 2023, 89, https://iastate.app.box.com/s/kiowofcpxnjbo89nh4qybykjrgb667q9.

69.   Ibid., 98.

70.   Ibid., 102.

71.   Ibid., 121.

72.   Ibid., 114.

73.   Ibid., 129.

74.   Ibid.

75.   Ibid., 95.

76.   Ibid., 119.

77.   Ibid., 124.

78.   Ibid., 114.

79.   Ibid., 55,117.

80.   Ibid., 102-103, 105-106, 118, 127, 135-136.

81.   Ibid., 106.

82.   Carrie Chapman Catt Girlhood Home, https://www.catt.org/.

83.   Scott Linford, "Review of *Woody Guthrie: American Radical*," *Ethnomusicology Review*, Volume 16 (2011), https://ethnomusicologyreview. ucla.edu/journal/volume/16/piece/467. The museum is silent about the fact that Guthrie never denounced Stalin and had major shortcomings as a husband and father. Guthrie never did anything for women's rights, yet the museum acts like he is the consummate social justice activist. I got a lot of flak when I talked to the museum managers about these problems. The Bob Dylan Museum is next door to the Guthrie, but I skipped out and drove to Kansas City for the evening after seeing so much "Hail Hail the Sacred Male." The Carrie Chapman Catt memorials and the Woody Guthrie Center are perfect examples of women's accomplishments getting highly underrated and men's accomplishments being dramatically overrated. Woody Guthrie was a great protest singer, and he was highly effective at raising consciousness on classism and racism, but we should not overlook or explain away his deep blind spots on sexism, misogyny, and Stalinism.

84.   Jane DeDecker, "*Every Word We Utter*: The Sculpture that Inspired the Women's Suffrage National Monument," https://everywordweutter.org/. The website is patronizing towards the suffragists depicted in the sculpture. They are not called brilliant, outstanding, innovative, ingenious, or heroic.

CHAPTER FOUR

1.   Chemaly, "Equality Day Is Meaningless."

2.   "4 Dorothy Height Quotes That Will Inspire and Empower You," Gender on the Ballot, March 24, 2020, https://www.genderontheballot.org/4-dorothy-height-quotes-that-will-inspire-and-empower-you/.

3.   Crystal Eastman, "Now We Can Begin," *American Yawp Reader*, December 1920, https://www.americanyawp.com/reader/22-the-new-era/crystal-eastman-now-we-can-begin-1920/.

4.   Allan G. Johnson, *The Gender Knot: Unraveling Our Patriarchal Legacy*, 3rd. ed. (Philadelphia: Temple University Press, 2014), 234. "The stubborn ounces of our weight" comes from Bonaro Overstreet's poem.

5.   Ibid., 240-242. The phrases "Make noise, be seen" and "Dare to make people feel uncomfortable" come from *The Gender Knot.*

6.   Elaine Weiss, "19th Amendment: The Six-Week 'Brawl' That Won Women the Vote," *Christian Science Monitor*, August 3, 2020, https://elaineweiss.com/2021/06/25/christian-science-monitor-centennial-special-coverage-19th-amendment-the-six-week-brawl-that-won-women-the-vote/.

7.   Ibid.

8.   Laura Bates, "Never Be the Most Feminist Person You Know—Laura Bates Meets Cynthia Enloe," *Guardian*, November 6, 2017, https://www.theguardian.com/lifeandstyle/2017/nov/06/feminist-laura-bates-cynthia-enloe.

9.   Alyson Krueger, "The Women Rethinking Marriage and Family Life Because of Miranda July," *New York Times*, June 8, 2024, https://www.nytimes.com/2024/06/08/style/miranda-july-all-fours-group-texts.html.

10.   Jill Filipovic, "The Tragic Irony of Feminists Trashing Each Other," *Guardian*, May 2, 2013, https://www.theguardian.com/commentisfree/2013/may/02/feminism-trashing-shulamith-firestone.

11.   *Her March to Democracy: National Votes for Women Trail* (podcast), 2025, https://hermarchtodemocracy.buzzsprout.com/2283722.

12.   "Olympe de Gouges, an Exemplary Symbol of Feminism and Humanism, Must Join the Pantheon," *Le Monde*, January 7, 2023, https://www.lemonde.fr/idees/article/2023/01/07/olympe-de-gouges-symbole-exemplaire-du-feminisme-et-de-l-humanisme-doit-rejoindre-le-pantheon_6156962_3232.html.

The petition to put de Gouges into the Pantheon is on this website: https://olympedegougesaupantheon.org/. To sign this petition, send an email to sylvia.duverger@orange.fr indicating your profession and place of residence. Put "Pantheonization of Olympe de Gouges" in the subject line.

13.   Aryeh Neier, "When the Student Movement Was a CIA Front," *American Prospect*, April 14, 2015, https://prospect.org/culture/books/student-movement-cia-front/.

14.   Jennifer Schuessler, "Amid the Outpouring for Ginsburg, a Hint of Backlash," *New York Times*, September 21, 2020, https://www.nytimes.com/2020/09/21/arts/ginsburg-feminist-backlash.html.

15.   Stephanie Coontz, *Marriage, a History: How Love Conquered Marriage* (New York: Viking Penguin, 2005), 148, 151. Kindle Edition.

16. Ibid., 281.

17. Eastman, "Now We Can Begin."

18. Coontz, *Marriage, a History*.

19. Nicholas D. Kristof and Sheryl WuDunn, *Half the Sky: Turning Oppression into Opportunity for Women Worldwide* (New York: Alfred A. Knopf, 2009), 191, 215. Kindle Edition.

20. Ibid., 259-261.

21. Ibid., 73.

22. Ibid., Chapter Two, 294.

23. Ibid., 75.

24. Ibid., 217-219.

25. "Fareed Zakaria Discusses the Modern Backlash Against Women's Progress," *The Late Show with Stephen Colbert*, March 27, 2024, https://www.facebook.com/watch/?v=7201422266619804

26. Fareed Zakaria, *Age of Revolutions: Progress and Backlash from 1600 to the Present* (New York: W. W. Norton & Company), 117. Kindle Edition.

27. Ibid., 352.

28. Ibid., 249-250.

29. Ibid., 249.

30. Zahniser and Fry, *Alice Paul: Claiming Power*.

31. Goodreads Quotes—Simone de Beauvoir, https://www.goodreads.com/quotes/10933775-humanity-is-male-and-man-defines-woman-not-in-herself.

32. Cynthia L. Haven, "C. S. Lewis, 'carny classics,' Joy Davidman . . . it all comes together," *Book Haven* blog—Stanford University, https://bookhaven.stanford.edu/2010/10/c-s-lewis-carny-classics-joy-davidman-it-all-comes-together/. C. S. Lewis fans are surprised to find he confided to his friend Sheldon Vanauken that he had married "to prevent the government deporting her to America as a communist."

33. Rachel Shteir, *Betty Friedan: Magnificent Disrupter* (New Haven: Yale University Press, 2023), 294. Kindle Edition.

34. Sheryl Sandberg, *Lean In: Women, Work, and the Will to Lead* (New York: Knopf Doubleday Publishing Group, 2013), 158-159. Kindle Edition. Sandberg should have lauded the suffragists and feminists' intellectual brilliance and she

should have called Alice Paul heroic. Nevertheless, this paragraph was a pleasant surprise.

35.   Keziah Weir, "Melinda French Gates Embraces a New Era and Gets Political—Even When It's Uncomfortable," *Vanity Fair*, September 11, 2024, https://www.vanityfair.com/style/story/melinda-gates-interview-politics.

36.   Ibid.

37.   Ellie Reynolds and Michelle Wellington, "Smithsonian American Women's History Museum Marks Women's History Month with More Than $55 Million in Donations," *Smithsonian*, February 27, 2023, https://www.si.edu/newsdesk/releases/smithsonian-american-womens-history-museum-marks-womens-history-month-more-55.

38.   Emma Hinchliffe and Joey Abrams, "The Share of Fortune 500 Businesses Run by Women Can't Seem to Budge Beyond 10%," *Fortune*, June 4, 2024, https://fortune.com/2024/06/04/share-of-fortune-500-businesses-run-by-women/.

39.   Emily Peck, "At the CEO Level, Women Finally Outnumber Men Named John," *Axios*, April 27, 2023, https://www.axios.com/2023/04/27/women-men-ceo-sp500.

40.   Kristof and WuDunn, *Half the Sky*.

41.   Julie Walton Gammage, *Quest for Equality: An Historical Overview of Women's Rights Activism in Texas, 1890-1975* (PhD dissertation, North Texas State University, Denton, Texas, August 1982), 40. https://digital.library.unt.edu/ark:/67531/metadc331239/m2/1/high_res_d/1002782390-Gammage.pdf.

42.   Jane Y. McCallum, "Texas Originals," Humanities Texas, https://www.humanitiestexas.org/programs/tx-originals/list/jane-y-mccallum.

43.   Jane Y. McCallum, Wikipedia, https://en.wikipedia.org/wiki/Jane_Y._McCallum.

44.   Natalie Proulx, "19 Ways to Teach the Nineteenth Amendment," *New York Times*, September 17, 2020, https://www.nytimes.com/2020/09/17/learning/lesson-plans/19-ways-to-teach-the-19th-amendment.html.

45.   Kelsie Brook Eckert, *Teaching Women's History: Breaking Barriers and Undoing Male Centrism in K-12 Social Studies* (New York: Routledge, 2025), 168.

46.   Ibid., 115, 204-224.

47.   Ibid., 92.

48.   Ibid., 230.

49.   Ibid., 129.

50.   Barbara Hood, "OPINION: Reclaiming Women's Equality Day," *Anchorage Daily News*, August 24, 2023, https://www.adn.com/opinions/2023/08/24/opinion-reclaiming-womens-equality-day/.

51.   Neda Ulaby, "Susan B. Anthony Museum Rejects President Trump's Pardon of the Suffragist," National Public Radio, August 20, 2020, https://www.npr.org/2020/08/20/904321406/susan-b-anthony-museum-rejects-president-trumps-pardon-of-the-suffragette.

52.   Nancy Goldstone, "I'm a Historian and I Think Women's History Month Is a Mistake," *Time*, March 23, 2018, https://time.com/5209670/historian-against-womens-history-month/.

53.   Sarah Stankorb, "The Christian Nationalist Plot to Disenfranchise Women Voters," *New Republic*, February 21, 2025, and Amanda Marcotte, " 'A Woman Is Like a Child': MAGA Quickly Turns Its Sights on Stripping Republican Women of Power," *Salon*, February 26, 2025, https://newrepublic.com/article/191420/christian-nationalism-save-act-voter-suppression and https://www.yahoo.com/news/woman-child-maga-quickly-turns-105907677.html.

54.   David Marchese, "The Interview: Curtis Yarvin Says Democracy Is Done. Powerful Conservatives Are Listening," *New York Times*, January 18, 2025, https://www.nytimes.com/2025/01/18/magazine/curtis-yarvin-interview.html.

55.   Ibid.

EPILOGUE

1.   Chloé Zhao, acceptance speech for winning Best Director for *Nomadland* at the British Academy Film Awards, 2021, in "*Nomadland* Wins 4 BAFTA Awards, Including Best Picture," *CBS News*, April 11, 2021, https://www.cbsnews.com/news/bafta-awards-nomadland-best-picture/.

2.   J. Correspondent, "Gloria Steinem Takes on Heavy Issues with a Light Touch," *Jewish News of Northern California*, April 2, 2010, https://jweekly.com/2010/04/02/gloria-steinem-takes-on-heavy-issues-with-a-light-touch/. The byline on this article, J. Correspondent, sounds like a pseudonym, and the name is not listed in the staff directory on the website.

3.   Katha Pollitt, "How Far Will 8 Years of Trump Set Back American Women?"

Nation, April 8, 2025, https://www.thenation.com/article/society/trump-women/.

4.   Margaret Hall, "Broadway's *Suffs* Disrupted by Protesters," *Playbill*, July 3, 2024, https://playbill.com/article/broadways-suffs-disrupted-by-protesters.

5.   Amanda Marcotte, "Mike Johnson Melts Down After House Proxy Vote Failure Exposes MAGA's 'Pro-Family' Lie," *Salon*, April 3, 2025, https://www.salon.com/2025/04/03/mike-johnson-melts-down-after-proxy-vote-failure-exposes-magas-pro-family-lie/.

Joanne M. Callahan is a women's history advocate who has visited women's suffrage sites throughout the country. She lives in the Dallas area and led the project to place a suffrage marker at Millermore Mansion in Old City Park. She has volunteered for the National Votes for Women's Trail for eight years and was involved in projects to place suffrage markers at the El Paso County Courthouse and Wooldridge Square in Austin. She recently retired from a four-decade career in information technology.